ABRAHAM
THE MAN AND THE SYMBOL

ABRAHAM
THE MAN AND THE SYMBOL

A JUNGIAN INTERPRETATION
OF THE BIBLICAL STORY

*Gustav Dreifuss and
Judith Riemer*

Chiron Publications • Wilmette, Illinois

Originally published in Hebrew in 1993 as *Abraham—Man and Symbol* [Avraham—Adam Ve'Semel] by Judith Riemer and Gustav Dreifuss. Copyright 1993, Ophir, Tel Aviv (TAG Publishers).

Translated into Italian in 1994 by Milka Ventura as *Abramo: l'uomo e il simbolo* by Judith Riemer and Gustav Dreifuss. Copyright 1994, La Giuntina, Firenze, Italy.

English translation prepared by Naphtali Greenwood.

Chiron Publications acknowledges the following for their permission.

"Isaac" [Yitshak] by Amir Gilboa. Copyright © 1963 by Ha'kibuts Ha'meuhad, Tel Aviv. Reprinted by permission of the publisher.

"The Binding" [Ha'akedah] by Mati Meged, trans. by H. Hofmann. Copyright © 1973 by Davar, Tel Aviv. Reprinted by permission of the publisher.

"No Ram in His Stead" [Ein Ayil Tahtav] by Ayin Hillil from *Ho'daya* [Thanks]. Copyright © 1973 by Ha'kibuts Ha'meuhad, Tel Aviv. Reprinted by permission of the publisher.

"Bequest" [Yerusha] by Haim Gouri from *Shoshanat Ruhot.* Copyright © 1966 by Ha'kibuts Ha'meuhad, Tel Aviv. Reprinted by permission of the publisher.

Cover: Painting *Abraham and Isaac* by Anton Van Dyck (1599–1641). Reproduction by permission of the National Gallery in Prague.

Library of Congress Catalog Card Number: 95–14100

Printed in the United States of America.
Copyedited by Carla Babrick.
Book design by Siobhan Drummond and Vivian Bradbury.
Cover design by D. J. Hyde.

Library of Congress Cataloging-in-Publication Data:

Dreifuss, Gustav, 1921–
    Abraham, the man and the symbol : a Jungian interpretation
of the biblical story / Gustav Dreifuss and Judith Riemer.
        p. cm.
    Includes bibliographical references and index.
    ISBN 0–933029–94–2
    1. Abraham (Biblical patriarch) 2. Isaac (Biblical patriarch)—Sacrifice. I.
Riemer, Judith, 1927–   . II. Title.
BS580.A3D74   1995
222′.11064—dc20   95–14100
                                                                                CIP

ISBN 0–933029–94–2

Contents

Preface

Gustav Dreifuss

For decades I have been absorbed by the story of Abraham. It came about like this: in the first years of my analysis, in the early 1950s, I had a dream about the division of an animal. This reminded me of Genesis 15, the Covenant of the Pieces, in which animals were divided as a symbol for the bond between God and Abraham. The dream and the amplifications helped me to experience and better understand the working of the psyche, of the unconscious.

The sacrificial act of dividing the animals led me to ponder animal sacrifice in biblical times and sacrifice in general. Why did ritual slaughter of animals exist? Why did people feel they needed to sacrifice to transpersonal powers? And what about human sacrifice? I studied the biblical text and the Jewish scriptures about the sacrifice (binding) of Isaac, which impressed me deeply. I then wrote my diplome-thesis at the Jung-Institute in Zurich (1959), "The Sacrifice of Isaac in the Jewish Legends" [Die Opferung Isaaks in den Juedischen Legenden], under the guidance of Sigi Hurwitz and Marie-Louise von Franz.

Living in Israel I was impressed by the collective remembrance of the Holocaust. In my analytical practice, working with victims who had suffered considerable psychic damage, I was again confronted with the archetype of sacrifice. In 1965 I published a paper, "A Psychological Study of Circumcision in Judaism," which was followed by many other papers on the subject of sacrifice, such as "Sacrifice in Analysis" (1977) and a paper on "Victims and Victimizers" (1984), published in Hebrew, to mention but two. The subject of sacrifice was continuously on my mind and finally found its expression in the writing of this book. In Judith Riemer I found a coauthor with an excellent knowledge of Hebrew and the Jewish sources. This book is the fruit of our mutual endeavor.

Dealing with this subject is an expression of my deep-seated need to experience and understand a certain aspect of the Jewish religion and culture from a Jungian point of view.

Judith Riemer

To be born in Israel means to be imbued with the stories of the Bible since childhood. One of these stories is that of Abraham, with all the dramatic events in his life, leading to the binding of Isaac.

Like every child who was brought up on the biblical story, I had conflicting feelings on this issue. I accepted, having no other choice, the pretext that this story had been told only to forbid human sacrifice. Yet living in this land means knowing the horrible suffering of parents who have to sacrifice their sons for the physical existence of the state in this hostile region. It means concretizing the archetype of sacrifice in the life of the individual and the collective in Israel. Almost no home has not lost a son in one of our existential wars; almost no one is not in one way or another connected with the Holocaust. Every Israeli is faced with the horrors of sacrifice.

The archetype of sacrifice is inherent in every individual and in every human society. On the extremely painful way to individuation, many sacrifices are offered. Sacrifice is not only concrete but also psychological, as old convictions, ideas, ideals, or neurotic behavior have to be given up for a new inner truth and understanding. Sacrifice is the price we pay for higher consciousness. Abraham's way to himself is a story of individuation; he is as well a collective human symbol.

Thus when Dr. Dreifuss suggested collaborating on the writing of this book, I gladly accepted the challenge of clarifying my doubts on the issue and suggesting a new meaning from the point of view of the weltanschauung of Jungian psychology. In it, cultural symbols are accepted as psychological concepts embedded in the individual psyche as well as in the collective one. Abraham is a symbol of one who looks for meaning, and Isaac is the archetypal sacrifice. The binding (sacrifice) of sons is a mythological theme all over the world. It is dealt with in Christianity as well as in Islam—only the names of the one sacrificed change. This story is relevant not only to the Jewish people, with its specific psychology, but has symbolic, personal, and collective meaning for all people.

Introduction

Readers will note that Abraham is often referred to as *Abram* in the early chapters of this book. As many will know, Abraham underwent a name change in his life—an event that is considered in chapter 5. As means of maintaining the integrity of an argument based on the evolution of Abraham's own life, his consciousness, and his relation to his God, we refer to Abraham as Abram when we discuss the character as he exists before the event of his name change. Readers will also note that Sarah is referred to as *Sarai* before the event of her name change.

—Gustav Dreifuss and Judith Reimer

One

Abraham's Childhood in Legends

Abraham, whose life, path to God, and path to himself are the sub-
jects of this book, is known to us only as an adult. The Bible provides us with no information about his early years. It simply presents
his lineage in terms of his direct descent from Shem, one of the sons
of Noah (Gen. 11.26–31). It is the adult Abraham who hears the
divine command, "Go forth from your native land" (Gen. 12.1). It is
he who is chosen to impart the belief in one God to the pagan society in which he lives and to beget a new nation on the soil of the
Promised Land. The biblical account gives us no information whatsoever about how Abraham was trained for this immense task. It is
no simple matter to assume the burden and attendant obligations of
being chosen.

The psychological aspect of being chosen—our point of departure and the basis for our discussion of this topic—is the experiencing of the Self. In Jungian psychology, the Self is that part of a person which is personal and transpersonal. Being chosen includes
listening to the inner voice that issues from the depths of the soul or
psyche—a voice experienced as that of the divinity. Summons and
command—in this instance, "Go forth"—are vital to the development
of the individual (the individuation process), for such a call determines one's aim, mission, and purpose in life. Summons, command,
mission, and thus the state of being chosen, all bring the individual
into contact with the transpersonal center of the psyche—the Self—
and express the person's uniqueness and obligation to consciously
carry out the mission. Through this consciousness the inner voice,
which imposes the mission on the individual and commands its ful-

fillment, is heard. Being aware of the demands of one's innermost voice means assuming responsibility for carrying out the commands, with all that this implies. Jung writes (1956, par. 459):

> In most cases the conscious personality rises up against the assault of the unconscious and resists its demands, which, it is clearly felt, are directed not only against all the weak spots in the man's character, but also against his chief virtue (the differentiated function and the ideal). It is evident . . . that this assault can become the source of energy for an heroic conflict, indeed, so obvious is this impression that one has to ask oneself whether the apparent enmity of the maternal archetype is not a ruse on the part of Mater Natura for spurring on her favoured child to his highest achievement. . . . "Mistress Soul," who imposes the most difficult labours on her hero and threatens him with destruction unless he plucks up courage for the supreme deed and actually becomes what he always potentially was. . . . The task consists in integrating the unconscious, in bringing together "conscious" and "unconscious." I have called this the individuation process.

Only a highly courageous individual can hear such a voice and heed its commands without repressing it, without evading the responsibility it imposes. Only a great individual can cope with a demand unparalleled in history and alien to his world. Only such an individual can convey to the world the message of belief in one God—an individual endowed with such personal strength, and such total conviction of the truth that issues from the innermost depths of his being. In other words, Abraham is an archetype, the collective symbol of the believer. He is the one who hearkens to and obeys the inner voice emanating from his psyche. His personal life, his trials and ordeals, speak directly to us and help us identify with him as an individual, a man, a father, and a lover who has become a symbol. Our interest in him helps us know ourselves.

To acquaint ourselves with someone, we need information on that person's development from childhood to maturity. The biblical account of Abraham provides no such information. To acquire a psychological understanding of the development of someone's personality, we need information and historical details. When and where was this person born? Who were his parents? What sort of childhood did he have? what joys? what crises? How was he educated? What was his social status? In Abraham's case, we must consider how these factors made him the right person for the mission that was imposed on him. How did his personal development, both conscious and unconscious, lead him to the conclusion that culminates in the biblical account and the command to "go forth"?

The Sages (see their work—the *aggadot*—as collected from the Talmud and Mishna in Bialik and Ravnitzki 1951) dwelled on this lacuna. With a profound psychological understanding of the human need to identify with heroic figures, they supplied the details of Abraham's early years in their *aggadot* ("legends"; sing., *aggadah*). Aware of the magnitude of the task assumed by Abraham, the narrators laid the foundations for a child prodigy who, in due time, would be capable of assuming great burdens. A person of miraculous birth, Abraham's adolescence is marked by wonders and acts of almost supernatural bravery, as in all myths designed to signal, through the child hero, the future adult's prodigious feats.

Myths play the role of a commentator, as Malinowski has noted. Myths express a living reality accompanied by the belief that such events actually occurred in ancient times and affect humanity in the present; they also articulate a reality that is both sublime and significant, one that determines the course of events and provides motives for norms of religious and moral behavior (*The Hebrew Encyclopedia* 1957, s.v. "myth"). In discussing the psychological aspects of myths, Jung wrote: "The myth is a natural and essential interim stage between conscious and unconscious cognition. . . . The myth is an expression of the collective unconscious" (1973, p. 311). The Sages made use of the myths of their time, reconstructing some for their own purposes and transmitting others with the emphasis prescribed by their monotheistic outlook.

As depicted in the *aggadot* (Bialik and Ravnitzki 1951), Abraham's childhood resembles that of many other mythical heroes, whose conception generally is miraculous and whose birth is characterized by wonders, such as a barren woman bearing a child (as in the biblical account of the birth of Isaac) or conception contrary to the laws of nature (as in accounts of the birth of Buddha and Jesus).

The newborn is immediately engulfed in dangers that result from the prophetic dreams of parents or others (often ruling figures). This occurs because these figures are archetypes who manifest themselves in powerful individuals who are capable of exerting influence and changing lives by virtue of their authority, which derives from their heroic status, ethical behavior, scholastic achievement, and physical strength. Examples are the prophecies of astrologers, as in the account of the birth of Oedipus, or a terrifying cosmic event, such as the appearance of a comet, as in the account of the birth of Jesus, and many more.

> When our Patriarch Abraham was born, a star stood still in the east and swallowed four stars at the four points of the compass. (Bialik and Ravnitzki 1951, pp. 23–32)

In one of the *aggadot*, Nimrod, ruler of Ur of the Chaldees, is told that the son born to Terah (Abraham's father) "will inherit this world and the world to come" (ibid). This news terrifies Nimrod and his astrologers and compels Terah to hide the child in a cave for three years, with the Almighty sustaining and educating him (Bialik and Ravnitzki 1951, Ma'asei Avot 6). The *aggadot* about Abraham's childhood have to be understood through the symbols in the stories that represent archetypes. By interpretations of the symbols, it is possible to acquire considerable knowledge of the hero's character and aims and of those who wrote the myths. A symbol is generally considered to be something that we cannot define by words alone. To understand it we need the analogies, amplification, and associations that accompany the hidden meaning. The *Concise Oxford English Dictionary* defines *symbol* as follows:

> Something that stands for, represents, or denotes something else (not by exact resemblance, but by vague suggestion, or by some accidental or conventional relation); *esp.* a material object representing or taken to represent something immaterial or abstract, as a being, idea, quality, or condition; a representative or typical figure, sign, or token (1942).

Thus far we have only briefly alluded to the *aggadot* surrounding Abraham's childhood. Let us consider two symbols—the star and the cave—that are significant throughout Abraham's life and which affect his development as an individual and an archetype.

In the first *aggadah* (Bialik and Ravnitzki 1951), a star stands still at the moment of Abraham's birth and consumes four other stars—a cosmic event that rocks the natural order of things. Here, the sun, stars, and all the celestial bodies symbolize order and unity amid the rampant diversity of the world. They are the rulers and leaders, the source of primeval life-giving energy, the symbol of the force that drives the world.

The domination of the other stars by the new star at the moment of Abraham's birth emphasizes the magnitude of the change that his birth will cause, a cosmic change that transcends the individual, an impending modification of the laws of Creation. The *aggadah* refers directly to the principle of order and oneness contained in the new weltanschauung, characterized by the impact of a new force, symbolized by a single star that subsumes the four stars that represent the ruling of the Many. This is the essence of the control that is exerted by the One over the forces of nature—the domination of the world by monotheism. According to the Sages, Abraham is the first representative and exponent of monotheism in recorded history (Bialik and Ravnitzki 1951, Ma'asei Avot 19).

Another symbol, one of the most common in myths and legends and perhaps the most important, is the symbol of the cave. (Consider the number of universal legends in which the hero, for one reason or another, spends time in a cave.) It is in the cave that the process of change occurs, during which the hero gathers his strength, determines his position, augments his faith, and emerges to tackle the challenges facing him. This process is the motif of rebirth.

The cave, generally portrayed as a circle or sphere, is the maternal lap on which the newborn rests. Caves are associated with the individual's origin as a fetus in the womb. As a symbol, the cave parallels the uroboros—drawn in the form of a snake with its tail in its mouth—a symbol of undifferentiated, unconscious wholeness. Any knowledge of it would violate its integrity, reducing it to its components, to a conscious differentiation of its parts and the awareness that each part of the whole is endowed with its own meaning and existence.

The *aggadah* has the child Abraham enter the cave as if returning to his mother's womb, to the loving lap that will shelter him from an unbearable reality—moral, religious, philosophical, or social—which points to a regressive tendency of the personality. He does not struggle with his difficulties, but in the cave, the refuge of this symbolic mother, finds the strength that will stand him in good stead in the future.

The retreat into the primordial state is temporary; it is a starting point as much as a need of the psyche to contact the unconscious in order to reach the conscious mind again. This is a rebirth, a rejuve-

5

nation of the personality, which is strengthened by new powers that direct it to the burden of the task it faces.

The return to the mother's womb—to the cave, the unknown, the darkness—is both fascinating and frightening. One is enchanted by the softly caressing and sheltering darkness, the unknown and unexpected. Confronting the fear encountered in such a womb-like cave leads to transformation of the personality, a numinous experience. In other words, one in the process of seeking full consciousness needs to deliberately walk in the wake of energy drawn from the unknown, which in turn produces the impetus for a continuous experiment to contact the Self. Instinctive knowledge, part of the process of consciousness, overcomes the fear of the unknown. This is the path of the conscious mind to the unconscious, which connects us to another meaningful archetype, that of the way.

Without realizing it, the Sages, in the *aggadot* of the cave, touched upon the motif of the way. There is an archetypal parallel of the voyage of the sun—the night sea-journey of the sun, with darkness all around in the cave. In the morning, light is born, and there is hope and life—and the person leaves the cave newly born (Bialik and Ravnitzki 1951).

Abraham's emergence from the darkness of the cave—symbolizing his rebirth—represents the beginning of his path, of his "going forth" and fulfilling his purpose in life. Removed from the protection afforded by the womb, Abraham, better equipped than at the time of his birth, walks toward light, awareness, and knowledge of the One, and toward assuming the role assigned to him in other *aggadot*—the role of an idol-smasher.

The motif of rebirth occurs several times in the biblical account of Abraham's life. In one instance, the descent to Egypt represents darkness and regression, whereas the departure from Egypt and return to Canaan—"with great wealth" symbolizes light and progression. The covenant itself functions as a symbol both of rebirth and of Abraham's conscious dependence on God. His ideal and aim in life are the source of his growing strength. Circumcision is a symbol of sacrificing the pagan world which is seen as darkness. Abraham's name change is an expression of his new and strengthened identity. The decisive change in his personality happened after the second command *lech lecha* (Gen. 22.2, "get thee into the land of Moriah"), which led to the Akedah—the Binding.

The *aggadot* contain additional symbolic motives, but we shall consider the significance only of the three years that Abraham spent in the cave as an infant. Stating the exact length of time, as the *aggadah* does, indicates that the child was sufficiently mature to cope with the world at the stage when he moves from his mother's authority to that of his father. In the *aggadah*, the cave symbolizes the mother and the light is emblematic of the father (Bialik and Ravnitzki 1951).

Of particular interest is the number three, which appears several times in the story of Abraham and symbolizes the first natural closed form: the triangle. The threefold repetition of what is said lends assertion, meaning, and strength, even without the magic feeling that the rhythm of three produces. The archetypal number three appears at every significant and dramatic moment in Abraham's life: the Covenant of the Pieces (a three-year-old heifer, etc.), the appearance of three angels heralding the birth of Isaac, and the period of three days granted Abraham between the time he receives the command to sacrifice Isaac and the actual Binding. Thus the *aggadot* explain how and from where Abraham—the man who became the archetypal symbol of the divinely commanded believer venturing into the unknown—derived his strength.

Genesis 12 opens with God's command to Abram: "Go forth" (to the most significant voyage into yourself and the world). What is the significance of this command? Whence does it emanate? How does it make itself heard? "And the Lord said to Abram . . ." (Gen. 12.1). While we will refrain from exploring the question of the substance of divinity, in our view the divinity does not possess human features, such as a mouth, ears, and nose. The divinity therefore cannot engage in speech. The use of *said* and similar words is symbolic and metaphorical.

As we are bound by the text, we must ask why expressions such as *He said, He spoke*, and *He saw* are used with reference to God, and not merely as figures of speech. Whence did Abram hear these commands? The only answer we can venture is that Abram did in fact hear voices, as in every instance in the Bible where God petitions people. The voices originate in the person, who is, in effect, hearing himself. The inner voice rises and expresses itself through means he can comprehend: the sound of speech—or prophetic visions—the limited language of concepts available to him.

The voice of the command, identified in the Bible as the voice of God, is, in fact, the voice of the Self. The command emanates

7

from the core of Abram's unconscious personality. The Self is the major archetype, providing equilibrium and regulation, imparting strength, and acting as the driving force—also as a braking and impeding force—behind a personality. The Self is the abode of the personal and collective energies that act upon and activate an individual—energies that include both consciousness and unconsciousness, manifesting themselves as will in the conscious realm and as impulse in the unconscious realm. Therefore, the voice of God heard by Abram is the voice emanating from within himself, from his unconscious. God spoke and was heard within Abram's soul.

"Go forth from your native land and from your father's house to the land that I will show you" is the divine command that Abram hears. It tells him to abandon everything familiar and venture toward the unknown. The change that the voice within demands of Abram must be total, for the inner change—Abram's ability to hear the command—demands that he make an outward change in his physical and social surroundings. Whether or not the purpose of this change is, as the Sages understood it, belief in the oneness of the conduct of the world's affairs and the imperative of disseminating this truth throughout the world, Abraham's innermost self insists that it be so.

Perhaps such a change could not occur in a setting governed by laws that conflict with the intrinsic truth expressed in the voicing of the command, the voice that arises from the Self. "Go forth" is heard because every process of development and change calls for dissociation from the past, from previously acquired concepts, from axioms that are no longer valid, and from a society fettered by ethical, religious, social, and psychological norms. "Go forth," the voice insists, into yourself—heed the voice that emanates from within you.

But does one have to disengage physically from the place of one's youth to effect an inner change? Can a new belief system develop in an old sociocultural milieu? There can be no absolute answer, for the simple reason that the psychological makeup and the personality of each individual must be taken into account.

In Abraham's case the answer is simple: he makes a clean break with his traditions and previous way of life. The change required of him is simply too great to permit any contact with his past. His environment, associations, experiences, weltanschauung, and the way of thinking that guided and directed his actions now constrain him, chaining him to the old setting. To break free, he must separate totally from his emotional and cultural background to accommodate the innate creation emanating from his new experiences.

Perhaps such a separation is necessary to reduce the likelihood that he will regress at times of weakness, pressure, and desperation to his reliance on familiar patterns of thought and behavior. The Abraham of the Bible is a human being who experiences difficulties, stress, and conflicts. He is, at the same time, both strong and weak. As we will demonstrate, Abraham regresses in order to progress—from a regressive state he emerges stronger and more secure in his beliefs; he never falls back into his previous, pagan patterns of behavior.

The command "Go forth" is the manifestation of a creative personality's search for itself, in transcendence of social norms. Abraham must seek a soil that is suited to the cultivation of this new creativity—soil that will nourish his creative activities and not chain or fetter him beyond the limits of his inescapable duties. In this way he is free to create for the sake of creation and to uphold the rules that derive from the laws that govern creation.

In terms of our weltanschauung, Abraham's disengagement from the past, as presented in Genesis 12, does not occur randomly. It proceeds from the emotionally relatively easy—"from your country" to the more difficult—"from your homeland" and the most difficult and meaningful change in a person's life—"from your father's house."

The "father's house" symbolizes the collective masculine principle of security and honor, family continuity, and tradition passed on from father to son. It stands for the weltanschauung grounded in the collective experience of the family: the mutual responsibility of family members and the ability of the collective to protect its members and face a hostile world. It also symbolizes conformity and conservatism; as the protector of its weaker elements, it cannot, by definition, tolerate shock, rebelliousness, or innovation. The patriarchal household functions as a rigid hierarchy. It demands absolute submission, which negates individual personalities. Anyone who desires individuation will not find it a compatible environment.

The personality that is driven toward change and development—toward individuation and personal wholeness—must break free of this setting. Development is a dynamic process. Its opposite is "your father's house"—the stagnation and rigid laws that are an existential necessity for its well-being. Abram, who destroys his

9

father's idols, is forced out of the paternal nest but is not yet free of his past. His father, Terah, begins the journey with his family, migrating as far as Haran, the gateway to the new land. However, since Terah is a symbol of the "paternal home," he must die in Haran so that Abram can enter Canaan, liberated from his past. Once in Canaan, Abram also takes leave of Lot, thus completing his break with the past.

Although Terah, in his capacity as head of the household, led the journey to Canaan (migration being the hallmark of nomadic society), his journey involves no vision whatsoever; he migrates in search of sustenance. This may explain why he is unfit to enter Canaan. His journey is not a quest for meaning. Whereas Terah wandered, Abram followed the Voice—obeying a compulsive need to advance toward new content and meaning that will develop in the new country.

One of the Hebrew words for *country* in Genesis 12—*moledet* (motherland)—is a derivative of the verb root *Y-L-D* ("to bear" or "to beget"). It symbolizes the collective feminine principle, the archetypal mother, who creates life and nurtures people. *Moledet* is man's natural home. A *beit av* ("one's father's house") in the motherland represents an integration of both the masculine earthly (as opposed to the masculine spiritual) principle and the feminine earthly principle.

Other terms—*eretz*, or *adama* ("land, earth"; also "country")—also symbolically embody the spiritual element. *Eretz* is a broad, abstract concept devoid of geographical, political, or physical borders, as reflected in the Hebrew expression for the globe—*kadur ha-aretz* ("globe of land"). *Eretz halomot* ("a land of dreams") describes a place where people are free to dream; *eretz ha-behira* ("the land of choice," or "chosen land"), is where one's desires and hopes are fulfilled and to which one's aspirations and yearnings may be attached. People do not choose the place where they are born, their *moledet*; an *eretz behira*, however, has various spiritual connotations that we project onto it.

Linguistic analysis of these Hebrew words may not conform to the intentions of the author of the biblical account. They may simply be a string of synonyms for a single concept. We believe, however, that the author of the biblical account knew the special significance of each term. The linguistic form is terse, almost laconic, and unembellished, unlike later poetic and prophetic passages. The reader must assume that the words were chosen with care, and that they are neither interchangeable nor rhetorically decorative.

Abram's inner voice leads him to "the land that I will show you," where the new creative force and the spiritual process gestating within his psyche can acquire their hoped-for final form. There, unrestricted by the old ways, these new capabilities will be nurtured and will flourish. In other words, Abram takes himself to a place where the internal process of change is reinforced and encouraged, to a sympathetic environment unfettered by memory. There the individuation process can magnify Abram's ability to heed the inner voice, which the biblical account identifies as the voice of God.

Canaan is the land chosen to nurture Abram the individual, who is undergoing psychic processes that forge and shape his new personality. Canaan also provides an environment where Abram the symbol may grow—an environment where, as a result of his psychic experiences, a new weltanschauung and faith—monotheism—are born. The father of a new people emerges, as promised in Genesis 12.

Is there reason for choosing Canaan as the *moledet*, the birthplace, of the new spiritual principle, apart from its being located in an area that is convenient for the migrations of Abram's family? Perhaps it was chosen because it is a natural crossroads, a convenient setting for the dissemination of the great message contained in Genesis 12. We believe, however, that it was chosen for what it does *not* contain, that its advantage is what it lacks. Canaan is not a soft, luxuriant country; it is most assuredly not a "land of milk and honey." Continuously conquered by the great armies from the south and north (Egypt, Assyria, Babylonia), it was a place that enabled a new truth to be spread. From its conquerors it absorbed cultural values and forms of belief. By living under constant pressure, the people developed a new weltanschauung, which Abraham represents.

Canaan is a waterless land that lacks the natural resources that attract human beings. It is a country so dry, hot, and windswept that Moses' spies accused it of "consuming its inhabitants." Perhaps the land was chosen to test human willingness to sacrifice and persevere in the face of deprivation, hunger, and thirst—in order to challenge human courage and the limits of endurance so that Abraham's descendants may appreciate the land's uniqueness and spiritual significance. Only such a hard and cruel country could be the setting for such tasks. Only there could be built the altar on which Abraham

11

binds his son in sacrifice to God. In a land such as this, the human scale of values as well as the meaning of land, *eretz*, are changed. As it is said in Hebrew: "The land of Israel is possessed only through agonies."

The afflictions suffered by the inhabitants of such a land represent a process of choice, as it were, between material and spiritual values—between those who can withstand the ordeals inflicted upon them and those who fail and depart. Like so many others, Abram stumbles, but he returns because his destiny so dictates. Afflictions are an inseparable and, perhaps, indispensable part of the process of personal development. Attempts at self-fulfillment and personality development must inevitably pass through the kiln of experiences such as Abraham's. This forging of the personality is the only way to achieve full human development: a very painful way, known as the process of individuation, which is an attempt by the individual to attain one's own innate truth, to arrive at the source of the strength within one's soul, to achieve the Self.

The Self demonstrates its presence within the individual, but it is also general and eternal. As such, it is enlarged in a process that may be called the individuation of a nation and of humanity. It is a process of development leading to increased consciousness and self-fulfillment within one's society. One of the manifestations of this process is a change in image of the divinity—any divinity. Insofar as the individual is part of the whole and is influenced by it, so, too, is society influenced by the individuals who comprise it. These processes of growth and refinement, the experiences and afflictions that affect individuals and lead them to heightened consciousness, affect the collective as well, albeit at a slower pace. Such heightened consciousness is the meaning of Israel's state of being chosen, as well as the meaning of its suffering. The process of individuation, which involves both a concentration of inner forces and a struggle to reveal the boundaries of one's personality, at times forces the person to leave society, often for the desert, either actually or symbolically, as Moses and other prophets did, or for unknown terrain, to return later with renewed psychic powers and a new set of values.

The process of individuation contains the very real danger of self-aggrandizement, of inflation, of feeling superior to and disdaining others, who ostensibly are inferior and unworthy. However, the suffering that accompanies the process offsets the individual and collective peril, which is part of the state of being chosen and the feeling of separateness that result from the process. Being chosen must be understood as a duty, a mission that brings much suffering in its wake. Modesty and humility entail a perception of the correct proportion between the personal aspects of one's aims and achievements and the suprahuman—the collective spiritual—dimension. The unceasing struggle with suffering obviates the danger of the chosen one deeming herself equal in prerogatives to the forces that chose her, even if they arise from within herself.

Thus Abraham becomes the symbol of suffering. Abram himself must experience all of the torments of humankind, as in the *aggadah* that recounts the ten ordeals to which he is subjected. Further examples are his anguish at having failed to stay in the land destined for him, as well as the collective future torment of his descendants (cf. Gen. 15.13). Abraham thus may be viewed as the prefiguration of all the suffering and afflictions, the trials and tribulations, that affected and continue to affect people as individuals and the Jews as a collective.

Guided by the divine command, Abram reaches Canaan but finds it inhabited: "The Canaanites were then in the Land" (Gen. 12.6). He continues to migrate, even in the Promised Land. The time is not yet ripe for permanent settlement, and he is not ready to sink deep, lasting roots into the soil. The union between this people and the land has not yet occurred, and so Abram continues to wander. Throughout Genesis 12, Abram not only fails to establish permanent residence anywhere; he even goes down to Egypt. These wanderings symbolize uncertainty and vacillation—Abram's search for the Self. His vacillation may be construed either as a manifestation of restlessness or as a way of familiarizing himself with the country.

The migrations indicate a lack of confidence and belonging, even in a nomadic society. The capacity for cross-fertilization seems nonexistent at this point. Abram must refine himself, purifying himself by further ordeals, before he can say, "This is mine." However, he never says this. Rather, he asks repeatedly, "How shall I know that I am to possess it?" (Gen. 15.8). He does not experience the Promised Land as his; he even purchases Sarah's burial place for cash from Ephron the Hittite.

Abram never takes possession of the land by virtue of his promise and right of ownership. He is unable to effect his right to the land and possess it because the land is already inhabited and cannot sustain him. We therefore begin to doubt whether the promise of the land to Abram was a literal one, or whether it was made in the symbolic, spiritual sense.

The Bible does not allude to such doubts. Although the biblical Abram asks questions, he neither expresses uncertainty about the rightness of his path nor complains about the promise given him that cannot be fulfilled. Nevertheless, it is reasonable to assume that he does experience doubt, given the reality with which he is confronted.

Abram, who hears and obeys the inner voice—the divine promise—faces a reality that conflicts with the promise of the inner voice. There is famine in the land, so Abram decides to go down to Egypt. The inner voice does not protest. It is a healthy instinct—the concrete ego that attends to the body's needs—that guides Abram's actions in accordance with the will to live and the existential imperative. Once this dominates his thoughts, Abram does not vacillate and the inner voice falls silent. Ethical considerations and the psychic quest are shunted aside. Abram performs as an uninhibited, realistic man of action. He lies when lying is necessary to save life, and does not hesitate to choose life, even at the price of leaving the land and handing his wife over to Pharaoh's court.

Abram does not experience any ethical vacillations; at least, the biblical account does not refer to any. The inner voice—the divine command—does not make itself heard in opposition to his course of action. Abram lives by the eternally valid laws of existence. The inner voice neither interferes with nor dictates the ethical response that we would expect, such as reminding Abram that Sarai is his wife. Had he practiced the accepted ethical precepts of today— behavioral criteria befitting an individual of his stature—such a proclamation might well have consigned him to death. The biblical account reports that Sarai was "very beautiful" (Gen. 12.14). The Egyptians' preference for immediate gratification of their desires for beautiful women would have brought about Abraham's end. He knows the norms of his society and decides to act accordingly.

Discretion and ethical judgment (as an overarching principle) are entrusted to God, who, in this instance, punishes Pharaoh for overstepping the bounds of accepted interpersonal ethics. However, this sublime ethical principle, of which God is custodian, changes over time, as does the concept of the divine essence. Pharaoh is nevertheless punished for violating an indisputable basic law of ethics—a supreme social command as valid now as then, since no collective can exist in its absence. These are universal principles, anyone transgressing them is liable to be punished.

When Sarai is taken to Pharaoh's abode as chattel, Abram, the pragmatist, forfeits his dignity. Life triumphs, overcoming wounded pride and tarnished love. It may be said in this case that normal ethical standards are waived when the choice is between life and death.

The account of Sarai's captivity in Pharaoh's court is one of the ten ordeals that afflict Abram mentioned in the *aggadah*. The Sages had no doubt that man cannot undergo such an experience without suffering severe psychic trauma. They understood the seriousness of the psychic injury incurred by Abram with the loss of Sarai, whether she symbolizes Woman as a component of his psyche—the anima, the feminine principle that influences a man's emotional development—or a flesh-and-blood woman, who is a symbol of wealth and status, or simply a beloved wife.

Abram's ordeal teaches us that consciously relinquishing dignity, property, and love can enable a person to attain such progress toward self-perfection that he gains direct access to the Self. In other words, through individuation, a person becomes capable of coping with himself and listening to his inner voice.

Two

Abraham—God's Command and Promises

Abram's pragmatism shows itself again in the biblical account of his parting from Lot. His relationship with his nephew-son having foundered, Abram is, for the sake of peace, prepared to forfeit his supremacy. Logically and with presence of mind, Abram decides to part ways.

The same approach guides Abram in his relations with others, which ultimately develop fairly and considerately. Common sense, flexibility, and the ability to abandon rigid principles serve him well in solving routine problems, as well as in more trying situations. Realism guides him in resolving the quarrel between his herdsmen and Lot's. Reasonably and calmly, he decides upon a split because of the shaken relationship between them.

After Terah's death, Abram, in his role of patriarch, has the right to render judgment and resolve disputes. For the sake of peace he humbles himself, allowing Lot to choose his own domicile. In taking leave of Lot, Abram relinquishes his power as patriarch, as well as his dignity, which in biblical times was judged by the number of persons and amount of property within the household. Later, despite the separation from Lot, Abram comes to his assistance, as blood ties oblige him, when Lot is attacked and taken captive (Gen. 14.12).

It is Lot who suffers as a result of his separation from the protection of the paternal house. Abram is perhaps diminished in physical strength by his loss, but his psychic integrity is not impaired, nor is his adherence to the internal principle that guides him: peace as an attribute that transcends physical force.

In psychological terms, the parting from Lot may be construed as a leave-taking from vestiges of Abram's past. It is a separation from something that represents the Mesopotamian way of life, tradition, and culture, from which Abram must make a break so that his innermost being may continue to develop. The old must make way for the new. As previously noted, any separation from any part of the past is as difficult and painful as any separation from parts of one's personality. Abram therefore needs the psychological reinforcement of the entity that represents the supreme authority for him—God or the "inner voice"—an inner conviction, expressed in the repetition of the promise "For I give all the land that you see to you and your offspring forever" (Gen. 13.15), with emphasis on the word *you.*

The promise given to Abram is phrased differently—"to your offspring" (Gen. 12.7)—as long as Lot is in his camp. After their parting, after the final break with the past, the promise is given to "you," to Abram, the person who has the audacity to embark on a new path. The promise is so phrased twice in one chapter, indicating that the reformulation is deliberate.

To emphasize and fulfill the promise, Abram is told to "walk about the land . . . for I give it to you" (Gen. 13.17). Thus symbol is transformed to deed. Abram's walking, his physical treading of a path, parallels the relationship of the victor and the vanquished, the proprietary attitude of the superior vis-à-vis the subordinate. Abram's feet conquer the land, which accepts his dominance. (Consider in this context ancient drawings and reliefs that depict victors applying their feet to the necks of the vanquished.)

Here, for the first time, the symbolic relationship between the psychic perception of the divinely promised land (Abram) and the substance (the soil itself) is effected. Spirit penetrates matter, endowing it with a significance that transcends mere matter. Canaan becomes a land with both physical and spiritual attributes, neither of which can exist without the other. This is the origin of its sanctity for Abram's offspring and their descendants. The idea sinks roots into the soil and affixes itself firmly therein. By treading on the soil, Abram himself is sinking roots—roots by virtue of which the land nurtures him and permits him to develop. He does not leave Canaan again.

The idea—the belief in one God, in unity—embodied itself within Abram. No spiritual idea—indeed, no idea at all—can exist independently of the body that bears it, forms it, and effects it. It requires a physical repository where it may be expressed and fulfilled. Thus it is that Abram the man—or a symbol of humanity—cannot exist without a "body," a venue endowed with the physical requisites. This is what the land provides him.

The symbolic walking on the promised soil marks a synthesis of the physical and spiritual elements. Every spiritual ideal, every human idea, needs a physical body in order to be able to manifest and express itself. Now that Abram has acquired a new dimension, now that the soil has become part of his innermost being, the principle of the soil having been absorbed and assimilated within his personality, Abram is ready for another encounter with the Self—the divinity—a different kind of encounter that will have tremendous impact on Abram's future. We speak here of the Covenant of the Pieces.

"Some time later, the word of the Lord came to Abram in a vision" (Gen. 15.1). The use of the word *vision* in the opening of this chapter of Genesis creates a peculiar atmosphere, one of tense expectation, as to the coming events—one that foreshadows a difference in Abram's next encounter with the divinity. The Hebrew word for *vision, mahaze,* is derived from the root *H-Z-H:* vision in both the straightforward and the prophetic senses. In its positive sense, *hazon,* derived from the same root and signifying "vision" or "revelation," implies an ideal embracing hope and redemption. In its negative sense, it means "false prophecy" or "delusion." The word *hozeh* (*contract*—a document setting forth an undertaking by its signatories), is derived from the same root.

The covenant between God and Abram is a contract signed in a ritual composed of the sacrifices offered in the account related in Genesis 15. A *hozeh* must embrace vision (*re'iyya*) and evidence (*ra'ayya*)—truth and testimony. Abram, witnessing and participating in the vision, becomes a seeing signatory to the contract. We believe that the author of the biblical verses was aware of and deliberately used the manifold meanings of the root *H-Z-H.* Previously, Abram has only heard the divine command; now, he both hears and sees it.

Because a vision addresses the senses of hearing and sight concurrently, it has greater power and effect; it also entails the participation of more components of the personality. The combined effect on the witness of voice and vision together exceeds the impact each of them separately.

In psychological terms, a vision activates conscious and unconscious strata in the psychic composition of the witness, which explains the influence it exerts, as well as how it was used in various religious ceremonies in the ancient world. Only with later cultural developments did visions move out of the orbit of religion to become a form and expression of culture in their own right.

Every *mahaze* includes some stage setting, however minimal, which is used to create the right atmosphere for the content of the drama. The vision also involves movement, plot, and dialogue among the protagonists in a conflict, which is usually the theme of the drama. Such dialogue may take place between individual characters, or it may be an internal dialogue between warring parts of the psyche, each taking a different side in the internal dispute. The plot is a dynamic process that ensues either on a physical stage or in an "arena" of psychic events, in other words, introspection. The plot progresses toward a climax—a crisis or watershed—and strives for resolution.

In the drama presented in Genesis, the curtain rises with God's proclamation, "Fear not, Abram, I am thy shield, thy reward shall be exceeding great" (Gen. 15.1). The divinity is attempting to soothe Abram and restore his self-confidence, which has been shaken as a result of his conflict with the five kings, even though that struggle was successful. Abram, however, needs more than promises of future protection and reward. He needs immediate support, the immediate realization of earlier promises issued but not fulfilled. As would any man, he longs for the promised son, whose existence will confirm and reinforce his selfhood. This is the aspiration, the pledge, with whose birth he will be able to effect his future existence within the new framework that is developing in his psyche. Bitterly he protests, "Since You have granted me no offspring, my steward will be my heir" (Gen. 15.3).

Thus Abram questions God's ability to keep his word and asks for a tangible sign that the promise will actually be fulfilled. Abram's doubts must be resolved by a dramatic act. His faith needs concrete psychological reinforcement, which is provided within the setting of the vision. The images he sees, the voices he hears, and the role he actually plays all convince him of God's omnipotence. The experience of his identification with these events and actions is powerful enough to overcome and defeat his doubts.

All this, however, is still prologue, rhetoric, a proclamation of God's intentions vis-à-vis Abram's pent-up remonstrances. Henceforth, God acts. The first act in the drama is set in the starry vault of Heaven that stretches into infinity before Abram. The mood changes as Abram is led by God: "He took him outside" (Gen. 15.5). Abram is no longer autonomous, arguing with God, disputatious and almost demanding—all conscious actions—but is passive, physically led by God, like a child in need of protection.

Abram's situation may be described as a realization of the link between two parts of the psyche, which some psychologists call the ego and the superego, and others call the I and Self. The concepts are proximate, if not equivalent. The difference lies in their underlying psychological weltanschauung. Here we invoke concepts that are scientifically inaccurate but nevertheless explain the subject, skirting the polemics between various psychological schools of thought about the components of the psyche.

One part of Abram's psyche represents the father; the other, the son. In this instance, the image of the son prevails. Thus Abram forfeits the autonomy he evinces at the beginning of Genesis 15, and is led, childlike, by the Great Father, who gains control over all components of his psyche.

This "Father" within Abram's psyche is not identical with the divinity, which is indivisible, unified, composed of infinite possibilities, and representative of the forces of existence and the universe. Rather, this is a personal Father, whom one can treat as one treats a human being. This Father is the divine image that is active within Abram's psyche. The limits of human consciousness make it impossible to grasp the infinite nature of the divine; the tools available to human beings are insufficient. Thus, an individual needs to project the abstract concept onto something within the realm of human perception. The divine image therefore is the form that the divinity assumes within the human mind. Jung defines it as a set of ideas of archetypal nature, which therefore must be seen as representing all projected energies. In most contemporary religions, the nature of the divinity is shaped by the paternal image, in contrast to older religions, wherein the maternal image held sway (Jung 1956, par. 89).

The notable characteristics of the "son" within Abram are passivity and docility—characteristics that require a considerable degree of unconsciousness. Nevertheless, Abram cannot entirely forfeit his active consciousness, as expressed in his request for a sign and a token from God the Father. In other words, Abram is full of doubt. God must prove his ability in fact; Abram still does not accept God's authority unquestioningly, as manifested, in the extreme, in the Binding of Isaac.

Abram's trust in God is not perfect and absolute, his faith still not free of doubt. Let us not forget that Abram himself plays a part in this vision. Such a player is within the sphere of the conscious, but is dissociated from day-to-day consciousness. Whether or not he identifies with his role, he is conscious of another experience—the experience that takes place only on the stage.

The forging of a covenant between a person and God is undoubtedly a numinous experience. Encountering the divinity is an experience that a completely conscious person cannot have. Abram, however, occupies a different sphere, an extraordinary realm that we may call an altered state of consciousness. In order to encounter the divinity, one must enter a state in which one is receptive enough to engage the deepest layer of the personality, since it is this depth of self, in fact, to which one is relating. Such communication between parts of oneself is feasible because of the altered state of consciousness. In this state a person may establish direct contact with the archetypal, unconscious stratum of their psyche—the stratum that, in Jung's terms, speaks in pictures. As the level of consciousness descends, so the numinous encounter between Abram and the divine image, which ascends from the unconscious, is facilitated. This experience of the divine, of all-embracing selfhood, is terrible and menacing; at the same time, it also results in mental and spiritual elevation.

The exhortation voiced at the beginning of Genesis 15—"Fear not"—may apply more to this terrifying encounter than to any of Abram's encounters with any entity outside his own personality, such as the five kings. The account of Abram's struggle with the kings and the rescue of Lot from captivity may be construed symbolically as representing Abram's war with the agents of the world of idolatry within him and the rescue from their sway of some of the components of his psyche, as symbolized by Lot. Thus interpreted, the account refers to much more than a historical event. The psychological significance of this war is the liberation of that part of Abram's psyche that had fallen captive to the pagan world, of the regressive element within him, symbolized by Lot. This struggle continues throughout his life.

Throughout the human development toward consciousness, we repeatedly encounter the cardinal motive that drives the individuation process. The main problem is one's internal struggle with the tendency to regress—to the familiar ambience of bygone days, to the temptingly pleasant and comfortable world of childhood, and, in Abram's case, to the pagan weltanschauung. The struggle narrated in Genesis represents the victory of the new worldview that is nascent within him, but Abraham, because he is a flesh-and-blood human being whose vacillations are symbolized by the struggle, will keep returning to and rejecting some point in his past, overcoming it, and then transcending it in pursuit of his goal. This is the dynamic of development and changeability that the individuation process, with all its vicissitudes, entails.

In our view, the Abram who undergoes this numinous experience (the Covenant of the Pieces), who participates actively in vision and drama, who moves from one state of consciousness to another, is completely different from the erstwhile Abram, although this Abram, too, has encountered God. Convinced of the truth of the divine command, his inner doubts excised, Abraham eventually is able to commit his son to death on the altar, as divinely commanded in Genesis 22. Such consciousness of the extent of divine power may well explain the trepidation that accompanies Abram's earlier encounters with the numinous.

The terrible and menacing element that one experiences when undergoing an inner experience during which psychic forces—innate attributes, instincts, and impulses—struggle with each other is the loss of control of the ego over psychic disposition, the domination of archetypal (unconscious) traits over the conscious personality. The individual finds her psychic equilibrium challenged; she loses her ability to function appropriately in the reality in which she lives.

A numinous experience is frightening because of the potency of the feelings it evokes and the personality changes it triggers. People fear the unknown; we feel safest in a familiar and known internal or external setting. The unknown includes change—a new consciousness, a different reality, a different personal experience. The return to psychic equilibrium after such a terrifying experience, which deepens and broadens one's consciousness, occurs when the characteristics of this experience are integrated into one's existing personality traits.

Abram absorbs the experience of this encounter and assimilates it into his personality; he thus achieves greater awareness of the existence of his relationship with God. This is the experience of the

23

Self, the archetype of wholeness that regulates the personality and which is experienced as a lofty, sublime force transcending the personality, the ego—a force such as God.

All of Abram's experiences of and encounters with God may thus be understood as an experiencing of the Self. We should now further explain the concept of Self that we have been invoking. Jung's writings refer to the concept often and in the following way:

> As an empirical concept, the self designates the whole range of psychic phenomena in man. It expresses the unity of the personality as a whole. But in so far as the total personality, on account of its unconscious component, can be only in part conscious, the concept of the self is, in part, only *potentially* empirical and is to that extent a *postulate*. In other words, it encompasses both the experienceable and the inexperienceable (or the not yet experienced). It has these qualities in common with very many scientific concepts that are more names than ideas. In so far as psychic totality, consisting of both conscious and unconscious contents, is a postulate, it is a *transcendental* concept, for it presupposes the existence of unconscious factors on empirical grounds and thus characterizes an entity that can be described only in part but, for the other part, remains at present unknowable and illimitable. (1971, para. 789)

This explains why Abraham eventually succeeds in fulfilling various unknown facets of his personality.

Since the phenomena of conscious and unconscious do exist, the Self as psychic wholeness is composed of conscious and unconscious aspects. In empirical terms, the Self appears in dreams, myths, and legends in images of an aggrandized personality, such as a king, hero, prophet, or redeemer; in symbols of wholeness, such as the circle, the cross, and so on. When it surfaces as a depiction of an integrity or reconciliation of opposites, it is symbolized by the essence of a united pair, as in yin and yang, two brothers, hero and villain, and similar polarities.

Empirically, the Self appears as the interplay of light and shadow.

> The archetype of the self has, functionally, the significance of a. ruler of the inner world, i.e., of the collective unconscious. The self, as a symbol of wholeness is a *coincidentia oppositorum*, and

therefore contains light and darkness simultaneously. (1956, par. 576)

Thus the "Self," the divinity, symbolizes wholeness; as a reconciler of opposites, it symbolizes man and the Universe. In terms of logic, this would be worthless speculation, were it not for its ability to empirically describe existing symbols and the names assigned to them. Empirical symbols often have numinous power and primary emotional value.

In sum, the Self as an inclusive concept embraces both father and son, and symbolizes humaniy's all-encompassing personality—in our case, Abram. The Self, as an active force in Abram's personality, is the father-son duo presented in the form of opposites coexisting within him. Thus when Abraham offers Isaac as a sacrifice to God, he is sacrificing one part of his selfhood to the other part: the personal to a personal God, and the self to the Self.

The experience of the Self is a mystical experience, made possible by psychic disclosure and a direct approach to the archetypal energy. The Self becomes visible in images we conceive. According to etymologists, *mysticism* is derived from the Greek root *myein*, "a closing of the eyes." The mystic closes her eyes to blind herself to both the physical world and the logical world of the intellect, turning herself over to unperceived forces associated with some other essence or existence. The mystic descends to the depths of her soul with the intent to effect a unity with the psyche of the world or of God, an emotional merger with the world. This is the origin of vision and revelation.

Jung defines mysticism as essentially a feminine receptiveness by virtue of its proximity to the unconscious. It is the unconscious that provides the experience of unity between the I and the Self,—God. Erich Neumann notes that mysticism is a dissolution of the ego into the unconscious. It is an elimination of the contradictions between the world, which is outside, and the man-I and the Self-God. Any numinous event includes the experiencing of God by the mystic, with a charge of energy that overcomes that of the conscious and can act contrary to and despite man's conscious will, even destroying him (1953, p. 9).

At this point, Abram experiences the unity of human and world in what is called *participation mystique*. Every action he carries out at this stage acquires the significance of a religious ceremony, of which the sacrifice is the climax. The covenant is concluded between person and God, between the inner voice emanating from his unconscious (the Self that commands) and the I, which is conscious, subdued, and dominated by the archetypal energy that emanates from within.

Since Abram is immersed in such a consciousness, he prepares for the ceremony which will conclude the covenant as God commands, by readying the animals and birds. God commands, "Take for Me"—take of what belongs to you, part of your Self, and render or consecrate it unto Me, which is the Self. To forfeit property that you own, that you love or need, and consecrate it unto God: this is the sacrifice, the forfeiting of a significant part of Abram's existence for the sake of a link with the Self in his existence—God.

The forging of the covenant is an act of mutual commitment; the sacrifice is the signature on the contract, as it were. A covenant is made between two parties who need each other for some purpose. Abram is interested in this particular covenant for obvious reasons. He needs a defender and a source of support to provide reinforcement and dispel doubts that have arisen within him, even though their solution will, in fact, come from within. God, too, needs the covenant. To be recognized and known in the world as a projected, amorphous ambience, God needs people of vision—in both senses of the word. Abram is such a person.

God promises—in a commitment that is repeatedly reaffirmed—to give Abram a son and an heir who will pursue the tasks and undertakings begun by Abram. God also confirms his promise of the land. In nearly every commitment to Abram, God reiterates the dual promise: Abram will become a great nation and he and his offspring will possess and dwell in the Promised Land.

It is *eretz* (land, soil) that facilitates the physical existence of humanity and has come to symbolize the body. Soil possesses feminine significance and substance. In *The Great Mother*, Neumann writes: "The land is the Great Mother, which gives life from within itself and is the source of all that grows. The fertility rite and the entire world's myths are based on this archetypal form" (1963, p. 48). The earth brings forth life. Every living thing is born from it and returns to it for burial. In death, every living thing becomes part of the soil, whereupon the earth brings forth new life, and so on in a process of constant renewal.

However, the intrinsic life-giving force of the soil cannot manifest itself unless it is coupled with the masculine principle through which this innate vitality is realized. This masculine principle is symbolized, *inter alia*, by wind and rain. The earth as an archetypal feminine symbol of the force of creation is expressed very clearly by the Hebrew: *adam* (man; Adam) is derived from *adama* (earth or dust). According to the *aggadah*, man was created from dust taken from the four winds of Heaven. Bear in mind that wind is a masculine symbol.

Hence the promise of *eretz*, of *adama*, alludes to Abram's fertility, which thus far has lain dormant. As will be recalled, only after the covenant between God and Abram is concluded and the sacrifices offered—sacrifices of great significance, as we shall see—does Abram's fertility manifest itself with the birth of Ishmael. It is, however, only after the sexual purification rite, the circumcision, that the significant son in his life—Isaac—is born.

Thus the statement that *eretz* equals *adama* contains multiple meanings. One is immediate, expressed explicitly by God. The other symbolically affirms the first, as alluded to in the very nature of the earth. The earth as a feminine principle also symbolizes Abram's precognitive pagan world—his life before recognition of the One God representing the spiritual masculine principle.

Abram's all-embracing personality accommodates both the unconscious feminine principle and the spiritual masculine principle. Living things, or, in this case, a new weltanschauung, can evolve only through the combination of both masculine and feminine. Perhaps this is why the two promises given to Abram—a son and heir, and earth, or land—are combined, for this is the proper symbolic integration of the two worlds, a synthesis that gives birth to something new, a change of form and thought, spiritual revitalization.

Three

The Covenant of the Pieces—Archetype of Sacrifice

The consecration of a covenant requires some ritual act that is sealed, as it were, by the offering of a sacrifice. The Hebrew term for the making of a covenant, *kerita*, alludes to the act performed. *Kerita* means "cutting," as in the action performed during a sacrifice.

The Hebrew for sacrifice, *korban*, is derived from the root *K-R-V* ("to bring nearer"), indicating the fundamental purpose of this ritual act. The aim of the sacrifice is to create a relationship between humanity and the divinity by offering an object of either actual or symbolic value. When the object of sacrifice is an animal, its slaughter represents the mystical relationship between life and death. The body of the sacrifice, ordinarily burnt on the altar, vanishes from the world as a symbolic surrogate for the person making the sacrifice.

Jung noted that all cases of offering sacrifice are in fact sacrifices of the Self, which manifests itself in the individual's willingness to give up that which is dearer than anything else, what is really important, to draw nearer to and establish a relationship with the Self/divinity.

The ancient practice of sacrificing sons—symbols of the continuity of the sacrificer's existence and future—is, perhaps, the best example of self-sacrifice. As retold by the Sages in the *aggadah* listing Abraham's ten ordeals, the deep-seated identification required between the sacrificer and the sacrifice reaches its climax with Abraham's willingness to sacrifice his son Isaac, with whom he undoubtedly identifies as if he himself is bound on the altar (Bialik and Ravnitzki 1951).

In his book *Symbols of Transformation*, Jung comments: "The

29

impulse to sacrifice comes from the unconscious" (1956, par. 660). Thus Abram must be aware of the magnitude of his sacrifice and has to carry it out of his own volition. Jung adds: "The libido [energetic] nature of the sacrificed is indubitable." (1956, par. 668, n. 70). This means that the act of sacrifice releases the energy pent up within the sacrifice, making it available to the sacrificer.

In other words, the offering of sacrifices is a system of give-and-take between humanity and God. The only exception arises in cases of total sacrifice, where the sacrificer expects nothing in return from God but makes the sacrifice out of complete personal devotion. An example of this is the near-sacrifice of Isaac, which we believe should be viewed as a self-sacrifice, similar to the self-sacrifice of a martyr. Although the latter term was not coined until the Middle Ages, absolute self-sacrifice—the renouncing of life for the sake of a religious or spiritual ideal, rather than abandoning an inner truth that is dearer than anything else—has occurred since time immemorial.

One who offers God a human or animal sacrifice is symbolically sacrificing the forces that characterize the offering. In return, the divinity provides protection with these symbolic forces, thus ensuring the person's present and future life. The offering of sacrifices thus exists on two levels: sacrifice as a need that arises from the unconscious, and the sacrificing of the immediate gratification for this need, which shows self-control.

Human development and maturation entail the postponement of immediate gratification for the sake of a goal that will be achieved in the future. The offering of a human or animal sacrifice characterized with special attributes and powers symbolically endows God with such powers. This helps explain why early divinities were depicted as men or animals. When people dedicate and transfer the power of a sacrificed animal to God, they are symbolically projecting this power onto the divinity so that the latter may invoke it to protect and thereby bless the sacrificer. This power transmission is the basis for the reciprocity that exists in the contract (*kerita*) that is entered into and concluded in the Covenant of the Pieces. It is a covenant (Hebrew, *amanah*) that stands for faith (*emunah*) and mutual trust (*emun*).

In subsequent phases in the development of humanity and faith, the sacrificing of animals may be seen as the human dissociation from an unconscious animal nature. By slaughtering animals and offering them as sacrifices, humanity may be seen as breaking away from the world of instinct and achieving greater consciousness.

Within this process, however, another need manifests itself—the need to purge the divine image of its bestial, instinctive components, with which it was previously endowed, and eventually extirpate these animal traits. Along the way, the gods lost their concrete image, instead becoming abstract expressions of the forces at work in the universe, with no need for actual manifestation.

Jung writes: "The sacrifice of the animal means, therefore, the sacrifice of the animal nature, the instinctual libido" (1956, par. 659). Perhaps this is why Abraham is provided with a ram in Isaac's stead in the biblical account of the binding of Isaac. Here the divinity/Self waives its previous need to articulate its bestial impulses and express its power in concrete fashion. Instead, it makes do with a symbol of power—the ram—which is sacrificed in due time.

It has been argued that the Hebrew word *el*, "God," is derived from *ayil*, "ram," a strong and mighty beast. It follows that the sacrifice of a ram to God is the sacrificing to God of the symbol of God. In other words, the ram—one part of the Self—sacrifices its aggressive aspect to God—the other part of the Self. The animals represent the unknown that belongs to the instinctual world, which has some sort of relative spirituality that is understood as the animal spirit and its soul.

It may be concluded that the animals listed below, each of which symbolizes a specific power and each of which is sacrificed by Abram in the Covenant of the Pieces, have a significance transcending the symbolic sacrificing of the instinctive, feminine world identified with idolatry. These animals, listed in a specific order with reference to each animal's symbolic significance—as valid today as ever—correspond to the cycle of human life. Each animal symbolizes a stage in a person's development.

Because it is a vague term, we do not deal with the word *meshulash*, the adjective that modifies the names of these beasts. Does it refer to a triangular mark in the animals' fur? to their age? We do not know. It should be noted, however, that the use of the word, a derivative of the number *shalosh* (three), is one of the archetypal linguistic patterns alluding to the imparting of power, strength, and vigor. The triple repetition creates a specific rhythm that is in use today as in biblical times, as, for example, in the account of Isaiah's consecration as a prophet (Isa. 6.3), using the words "Holy, holy, holy."

Of the five animals sacrificed at the Covenant of the Pieces, three are mammals and two are birds. The heifer, the she-goat, and the ram symbolize the earthly aspect of the instinctive world of animals, while the young pigeon and the turtledove symbolize its spiritual aspect.

The heifer symbolizes childhood, growth, and development. It stands for lack of autonomy and reliance on others—dependence on parents.

The she-goat symbolizes maturity in the feminine aspect of nature. She can feed herself and is independent; however, her independence is not deliberate and her development not planned. She is free, but has no defined goal apart from the instinctive drive to gain the immediate gratification of her needs.

The ram symbolizes maturity in its coarse, aggressive, masculine sense. It represents leadership in the world of senses and drives—the instinctive, natural, feminine world.

The turtledove symbolizes the spiritual masculine aspect of this world. It represents the ability to ascend and soar upon the achievement of the latter stages of maturity, followed by age and death.

The young pigeon symbolizes infancy and the regeneration of life following death. This is the life cycle in the world of the Great Mother, the end of which is tantamount to the beginning. Death dominates this world only on the level of the individual; the indivisible unconscious world lives forever.

The three mammals are rent into pieces. This act of division indicates curiosity and an attempt to comprehend their inner contents and symbolical significance. It expresses the aspiration to understand the secret of their strength and their manner of behavior.

It is of course possible that this action is simply reminiscent of a custom pursued by the priests of Babylonia, whence Abram came, to foretell an individual's future by examining the liver of a sacrifice he has offered. Be that as it may, it is also a manifestation of the human need to understand, comprehend, and know—to leave the world of the unknown for the world of consciousness.

The placing of one piece opposite or against the other symbolizes one's familiarization with the external and internal content of the sacrifice—a complete, all-embracing view and an attempt to reveal the operative agent that makes the sacrifice unique and lends it its characteristics, thus investing the divinity with comprehensive strength. The three sundered mammals belong to the material aspect of nature, and their treatment by Abram may attest to his attempt to reveal the animal soul, including its spiritual dimension. Perhaps the birds were not carved because they symbolically belong to the spiritual aspect of the world. The spirit cannot be dissected, it must be accepted whole, it should not be divided. It is one special entity, even though it belongs to the world of multitude. In the course of this carving, the representatives of the primeval female world pass from the domination of multiple idols to the control of the unitary, spiritual male god.

The two cognitive processes of examining and investigating expand consciousness. Carving—an act of partitioning, of reducing to detail—leads to an understanding of the unitary nature of the whole that is composed of these parts. Thus Abram, sacrificing these symbols of power, understands the proliferation of faces of the divinity and psychologically achieves an equivalent status, in the sense of being one who understands their existence within the divinity and grants them to the divinity. This is how God and Abram enter into the covenant; they are, as it were, "equals."

Abram sacrifices five animals. This figure cannot be coincidental, for the number five symbolizes people as they exist in nature (with a head, two arms, and two legs), unseparated and undifferentiated from the unconscious world of the Great Mother. Abram grows psychically and spiritually because his personality is an amalgam of elements of his pagan past, the new spirituality he has acquired, and traits not yet coalesced within him. His ability to sacrifice the symbols of his past to the new God gives him a wider human dimension, as well as consciousness of the existence of these features within him. He also sacrifices the symbol of being unconscious, a man of nature—the "five"—and this makes him more aware, separate and differentiated from the world of nature and its domination. His conscious personality is made up of both spiritual and corporeal attributes.

The feminine principle is assimilated into the masculine principle and enriches it. The new principle contains both the concrete and the spiritual aspects. Into the midst of a numinous vision imbued with a sensation of the transcendental experience of communion with God—itself a pronounced mystical experience—erupts a destructive force symbolized by the bird of prey. Thus the principle of the idolatrous spirit attempts to frustrate and undermine the covenant between Abram and the new divinity.

The raptor, like an emissary from the old world, tries to protect and preserve the values of the world Abram has left behind. It is a child of the feminine pagan world, which opposes the new masculine principle. It is a symbol that preserves the status quo and resists all innovation, all change, any development that may jeopardize the strength of its dominion.

Abraham protects the pieces, which symbolize the ability to change and the revolution that has already occurred and will continue to occur within his psyche.

The bird of prey, like the other animals participating in this vision, like God himself, symbolizes a part of Abram's personality and a force at work in his psyche—specifically, the stagnant, conservative facet of Abram's mind, which opposes and rebels against the changes taking place in it. Thus the bird of prey represents the regressive element in Abraham. It is the symbol of Nekhebit, a goddess in the ancient Egyptian pantheon, one of whose roles was to protect the dead in the underworld. This is why the bird of prey alights on the carcasses of Abram's sacrifice.

Our collective consciousness relates negatively to the bird of prey. However, the principle of "evil"—the raptor—has its role to play in the world in engendering consciousness of the war between the principle of the old and development of and receptiveness to the principle of the new. This war is symbolized by Abram's driving the bird of prey away from the carcasses.

The principle of evil does not have a single, unequivocal, and univalent nature. Rather, it is the result of ethical development determined with different cultures—codes that vary with the culture and its values. Because it is fluid, the principle of evil also symbolizes doubt. Thus, by driving the bird of prey from the carcasses, Abram is also dispelling his doubt in God, which was expressed at the beginning of Genesis 15. Once he overcomes his doubts, his desire to change nothing (since all change requires an effort, and young and belligerent strength), Abram falls into a deep sleep, a state of unconsciousness, a dream. The biblical account explains: "As the sun was about to set, a deep sleep fell upon Abraham, and a great dark dread descended upon him" (Gen. 15.12). Thus the curtain falls on the first act, and the second one begins.

In his dream, Abram is given both a personal and a collective message. In the personal sphere, he is promised that he will be gathered unto his fathers in peace; in the collective domain of his son's future, he is promised suffering and servitude—which nevertheless is accompanied by hope and redemption four hundred years hence.

Instances of prophetic dreams have been recognized throughout the ages. The Bible is replete with such dreams. Prophetic dreams are telepathic; their images and voices emanate from knowledge that exists in the unconscious. In sleep, when rational inhibitions are removed, when the barriers fall and the level of consciousness drops, images and messages arise from the "other consciousness," which in periods of wakefulness would not be able to cross the barrier of logical thought.

At times we relate to the unconscious in terms of its being the source of negative forces only. This, however, is not the case. The unconscious is dangerous only when unconscious, undifferentiated, undefined, and uncharacterized contents that possess considerable energy take over. In such circumstances, the actions of the individual are no longer controlled by his or her consciousness. The unconscious, however, is also the source of the energies that drive human beings to achieve. It is the source of the most deep-seated attributes—the archetypes that constitute aspects of the collective unconscious, from which the psychic energy that motivates us is derived. The archetype dresses itself in recognizable forms so as to be identifiable.

The first and most conspicuous form of any energy is fire. It is only natural, therefore, that fire should symbolize the greatest energy of all—omnipotence, the divinity, as in the biblical account of the Burning Bush. Fire worship is one manifestation of the human attitude toward this energy. It is therefore natural that "a smoking oven, and a flaming torch" (Gen. 15.17) should take the form of an omnipotent divine image passing between the pieces and effecting its hold over them, their attributes, and their symbolic meaning.

In sum, the Covenant of the Pieces presents us with an expression of two prerequisites for the development of humanity and faith—recognition of the many faces of God and, at the same time, recognition of the undivided whole as a single, all-embracing oneness. Carving and parting represent the division of components comprising a whole; the breaking down of a oneness; and cognition, on the conscious level, of the multitude of the parts and the intrinsic attributes of the whole. Being able to recognize the individual parts

35

of the whole makes it possible to reassemble the whole from its parts. Recognizing the fragmentation of which we are made and being aware of our multiple aspects makes it possible to sustain a diverse, multifaceted personality, rich in spiritual content, and able to take action—as close to the spiritual as to the corporeal.

Presenting the pieces, one facing the other, is a symbol of understanding the inner contents of things. It could symbolize the state of knowing the inner content of God without knowing its unlimited boundaries. As the pieces symbolize the known multitude, the Covenant of the Pieces symbolizes Abram's ability to recognize the multifaceted God. Thus, Abram's own complex being is expressed by the many animals he sacrifices. Such sacrifice symbolizes his conservative inclination, his servitude, his aggression, and his desire for spiritual freedom, tenderness, and reassurance. It symbolizes the man and his godly spirit. All these facets are of the energy of the central archetype, the Self—God—which regulates the personality.

Four

Sarah and Hagar

After the magnificent ceremony where the covenant between Abram and God is sealed, and after Abram's numinous experience, which, almost by design, returns Abram to human dimensions, offsetting the inflated personality he might otherwise have cultivated, the Bible describes the bitter reality of his life—a reality that is contrary to the divine promise, "To your offspring I assign this land." (Gen. 16.18). For Abram has no offspring. Genesis 16 opens with a reference to Abram's secret pain: "Sarai, Abram's wife, had borne him no children."

We embark now on a detailed discussion of Sarai and Hagar, Abram's wives. We do not deal with Keturah because she enters the picture only after the binding of Isaac, when Abram is a very different, more complete, person than the one who appears in the earlier chapters of Genesis. Abram's responses to the actions of Sarai and Hagar and his relationship with them are examined in terms of the biblical account. Our discussion encompasses the influence on Abram at this stage, of a particular component of a man's personality, that in Jungian terms is called the anima.

The anima is a set of female images embedded in the male psyche against a background of an archetypal structure. It acts as a feminine principle that largely determines a man's attitude toward women. The origin of the feminine principle within the male psyche lies in the personal experiences of the child and adolescent with his mother, as well as the feminine image dominant in the culture and society to which he belongs. The image is not static; it changes in the societal view of women and the man's personal experiences.

The anima is thus multifaceted, ranging from one's personal perception of his mother to the wholly imaginary, from the High Priestess to the lowliest female slave, from Sarai to Hagar.

The anima is essentially unconscious. It can be positive, making a man receptive to his emotions and to his creativity. When it is negative, however, it endangers him by subsuming his consciousness and dictating his behavior. One aspect of this domination is admiration for certain women, who become symbols that are either unreservedly venerated by society or unjustifiably cast out for lack of understanding and fear of the feminine. The anima exerts a powerful influence on the male for good or evil, frequently triggering far-reaching changes in his patterns of behavior and thought. Jung calls the anima the archetype of life.

Abram's anima has two readily discussed facets: Sarai and Hagar. Sarai and Abram are blood relatives: "She is my sister, but not from my mother's house." Sarai is the first lady of the family. She stands at the top of Abram's ladder of feminine psychic images, from which she derives the power to affect his behavior. He does respond to her demands and actions. Hagar, on the other hand, is the stranger, the alien, the Egyptian handmaid at the bottom of the social ladder, and Abram treats her heartlessly. As symbols of the anima, however, Sarai and Hagar both are flesh-and-blood women, with a broad range of emotions that affect Abram.

The biblical account tells us nothing about Sarai except that she is beautiful. It does not provide details that might shed light on her personality. We do know, however, that she is cursed with barrenness. Although she is a catalyst for significant events (in the course of which Abram shows himself to be, by modern ethical standards, pragmatic, inconsiderate, insensitive, and wily), Sarai's personality is not described nor is her voice heard. She is a tool that Abram uses as he sees fit. She serves as a sexual object for Pharaoh and, later, for Avimelech. She is completely passive. Abram does not ask her how she feels, but orders her, in order to save his own life, to go to the palaces of the rulers whom he fears. Let us remember, however, that all this is in keeping with ancient attitudes concerning the nature and role of women.

Abram behaves according to traditions prevalent in his society. Granted, he changes some behaviors characteristic of his day as a result of his special nature and mission, as he grows in new directions. However, his growth does not manifest itself in a change in his attitude toward women.

From this point on, the biblical account begins to paint a portrait of Sarai as a real woman—a woman with specific wishes, aspirations, and desires. Sarai presents a complex image of a tough, bitter, and cruel woman who is fighting for her honor and status, who calculates the most trifling detail.

Despite her great beauty, Sarai has not fulfilled her feminine mission, and this failing becomes a source of frustration and bitter disappointment. It may be that Sarai's barrenness is a result of Abram's inability to beget a son who will sustain his spiritual dynasty because his own spiritual outlook has not yet matured. He does become a father in the literal sense, however, when Hagar gives birth to Ishmael.

Barrenness—whether biological or psychological—is the body's inability to fulfill its natural function. It is a state that we often see as being in conflict with nature. The motif of the barren woman who gives birth to the hero appears throughout the Bible: Sarah, Rachel, Hannah the mother of Samuel, the mother of Samson, and many others. The role they play as mothers of heroes is to prevail over an enormous handicap, barrenness, in a symbolic preliminary act that alludes to the role of the hero when he grows up—to prevail over the natural course of events, to go against the current.

Sarai views giving birth to a son as a realization of her womanhood and the completion of her personality. A product of her time and faithful to her role, she views bearing a child as the essence of her feminine nature. Sarai does not necessarily want to provide a son and heir for Abram to assume the burden of his father's undertakings to God and himself: she simply wants to fulfill her biological destiny, to play her feminine role, to give it substance by having a son.

As long as Abram's family remains nomadic, searching for a site, becoming familiar with the environment (tantamount to seeking a path), the problem of bearing a child is not a pressing one. The feeling of security that settling down confers on a human being makes Sarai aware that she is not fulfilling her feminine mission. Her longing to bear a child is now verbalized. Perhaps she feels that time is passing her by. Afraid that she will no longer be able to bear a child because of her advanced age, Sarai expresses an urgent need to do something.

It was accepted practice in the period of the patriarchs that when the mistress of the house was barren, the handmaiden was given to the master in order to bear him a child. The most famous biblical handmaidens of mistresses who were themselves unable to bear a child were Bilhah and Zilpah, who were given to Jacob by Rachel and Leah. In time, these handmaidens acquired in the national mind a status that was almost equal to that of their mistresses; certainly, their sons had equal value and status with those born to the *de jure* wives. (This did not happen with Abraham's sons. Only Isaac is considered the heir to Abraham's dynasty.)

It seems that the biblical handmaidens, whose ethnic origins are not mentioned, were members of the family, perhaps relatives. This is not the case with Hagar; she is explicitly identified as an Egyptian. There is no obligation or tribal responsibility toward her, no blood relationship whatsoever. She was purchased, like a bull, donkey, or camel. The reference to her Egyptian origin suggests that she is a foreign body within the family that will eventually have to be uprooted from it and expelled. And because Egyptian has negative connotations in many biblical contexts, the judgment passed on the son of the Egyptian woman is that he be cast into the wilderness.

Sarai gives Hagar to Abram in the hope that she will be "builded up" through her. Thus "Abram hearkened to the voice of Sarai" (Gen. 16.2), that is, he complies with her wishes, but as an uninterested party. This may be inferred from the placement of this verse at the beginning of the chapter in which an unpleasant aspect of Abram's character is revealed.

Hagar is proud that she has become pregnant, something that her mistress has not been able to do. Being thus "swollen," both physically and emotionally, she rejects the yoke of slavery. She is sufficiently secure in her status as the one who is carrying Abram's heir that she does not bother to conceal her contempt for Sarai ("and her mistress was despised in her eyes"—Gen. 16.4).

In a society that measured the value of a woman by the number of children she bore, it is no wonder that Hagar saw herself as the future mistress of the family. A medieval commentator, Rabbi Shlomo Yitzhaqi of Troyes, known to us by the acronym Rashi, expanded on this in his interpretation that Hagar was the daughter of Pharaoh, destined to rule rather than to be ruled, and that her pregnancy was her way out of servitude (Rashi *Pentateuch*).

In the biblical account, once Hagar learns she is pregnant she becomes unbearable. Sarai is both angry and hurt. Pain and jealousy consume her as she witnesses the pregnancy of her handmaiden. In her desire for a son, Sarai foresees neither the changes that are likely to occur in Hagar nor what will happen in her own mind. While Sarai rails only against Hagar's arrogance toward her, it may be assumed that it is jealousy that leads her to treat Hagar so cruelly that Hagar flees from her into the wilderness.

Sarai is going through what may arguably be the most difficult time in a woman's life—the end of her fertility, which signifies the end of her feminine function. She knows that time is pressing, that if she does not become pregnant now she is destined to remain childless. She struggles here not merely with her overarching feminine destiny, as prescribed by her personal norms as well as by the norms governing her society, but also with the feeling of a woman who is cut off from the feminine principle as she perceives it.

Sarai also feels threatened by the loss of her dignity and status within the family, but she directs her anger at Abram ("My wrong be upon thee"—Gen. 16.5). She continues: "The Lord judge between me and thee." Has Abram harmed either Sarai or Hagar? We suspect that perhaps Sarai is complaining to Abram because he is, in her opinion, overly kind to Hagar, either because of Hagar's pregnancy or her relative youth. Whether or not this is the case, we must consider the reason for Sarai's complaining to Abram, and in such extreme terms. For it is Hagar, not Abram, who hurts and degrades her. Sarai, however, reminds Abram that it is only because of her that Hagar was given to him ("I gave my handmaid into thy bosom"—Gen. 16:5).

The phrase "My wrong be upon thee" helps us understand the helpless rage, the attribution of responsibility for the wrong done to Sarai, which—albeit in a veiled form—contains the threat of future punishment. Abram reacts with indifference: "Behold, thy maid is in thy hand; do to her that which is good in thine eyes" (Gen. 16:6). This episode reveals Abram in an unflattering light. It is as if he has withdrawn into a world where the ethical standard previously important to him no longer applies. The sense of moral judgment with which he has been graced vanishes in the face of his wife's arguments. Subject to Sarai's fury, he lacks all independent will and judgment. Even the fact that Hagar is carrying his son and heir lacks significance in his eyes. Perhaps the memory of his having asked

41

Sarai to go to Pharaoh's house to save his own life is what guides him here. He does, in fact, owe her his life. Abram appears powerless to deal with this memory, on the one hand, and Sarai's anger and jealousy, on the other.

It seems, therefore, that Abram's feelings of guilt affect and distort his good judgment. We must assume that when he advises Sarai to "do to her that which is good in thine eyes," he knows that he is abandoning Hagar, placing one woman's fate in the hands of another who is consumed by jealousy, fearful for her own position, and recently humiliated.

"And Sarai dealt harshly with her" (Gen. 16.6) is a logical consequence of the situation in which Sarai has become entangled. Abram neither interferes with nor assumes any responsibility for Hagar and her fate—at least the biblical account contains no such reference. Sarai is authorized to vent her spleen, and she deals with Hagar as her jealousy dictates. We may therefore assume that Sarai does everything she can to encumber Hagar and embitter her life. Sarai takes revenge on Hagar for her own outraged femininity, until Hagar finally flees.

Sarai seems to be utterly blind to the role that she herself has played in this drama, to the responsibility she bears for the situation by having given Hagar to Abram. She is the victim of her own desire for a son, having anticipated neither her own quite natural feelings of jealousy nor her handmaiden's happiness. She knows neither herself nor Hagar.

How could she not have known that Hagar, who has lived with and served her for quite some time, would behave arrogantly? How could she have failed to recognize the attributes of her slave's personality? The only explanation is that she herself is so arrogant that she is unable to recognize the slave as possessing—like any human being—her own will, aspirations, and hopes. Sarai is unaware, immature, and controlled by her impulses, unable to anticipate and analyze the consequences of her actions.

Hagar proves unable to cope with Sarai's cruelty. She flees into the wilderness, knowing full well that death awaits her there. It seems she has decided that death is preferable to such a life. The fate of a slave who flees from his master is death. So too the person who flees to the wilderness—especially a pregnant woman—faces almost certain death.

The desert must be construed symbolically. It is a place with a multitude of hidden faces, rife with danger, crawling with snakes and scorpions, where people are beset with thirst and possible death, and where springs of fresh water suddenly appear. To survive in the desert, one must marshal all one's mental resources, hone the senses, and muster all one's psychic fortitude. Those who are unable to do so are doomed.

The wilderness is a very effective symbol of the unconscious. What arises from the unconscious is as dangerous and frightening as the desert, but it also provides a solution to the person who is able to hearken to what comes from within, like a spring of water suddenly revealed. This challenging yet revelatory capacity explains why the desert has been a place of refuge not only for rebels and insurgents, but also for those upon whom society looks unkindly—those who need time for introspection to resolve problems that require psychic effort and concentration, purification, and understanding.

The biblical text shows that, as a result of her arrogance, which ill befits her status as a handmaiden, Hagar needs time for self-examination and introspection, beyond her impulse to flee from Sarai's harshness. She also benefits because she is able to hear the inner voice that guides her as it rises from her unconscious.

Even before the angel (the inner voice that speaks from the Self) appears before her, Hagar sits down to rest by "a fountain of water in the wilderness" (Gen. 16:7). The fountain here is a well, a spring, a conventional symbol of life, of the vitality that flows when water manifests itself in the desert. Hagar sits next to the water, unwittingly choosing life. The voice of the angel commanding her to return to Sarai—"Return to thy mistress, and submit thyself under her hands" (Gen. 16.9)—clearly indicates that she is making an instinctive choice, as symbolized by her sitting next to the fountain. The dialogue that develops between Hagar and the angel of the Lord is the internal dialogue that people conduct with themselves when they deliberate and then make fateful decisions.

One of Hagar's considerations, not referred to here, is that, as a mother-to-be, she is responsible for the new life developing within her and for giving her baby a chance in life. After all, it is through him that her personality will show itself to have significance and substance. All personal fulfillment and realization entail some degree of suffering. This is the meaning of the command, "submit thyself under her hands."

Hagar decides, with the help of the angel's command, the innermost voice, to return to the relative security of Abram's house, to swallow her pride, to submit and obey. She returns to Sarai for the sake of the unborn child. This decision may be regarded as proof of her having grasped the meaning of suffering. Hagar's life has value only insofar as it relates to the child she is about to bear. The angel compensates her with the promise, "I will greatly multiply thy seed, that it shall not be numbered for multitude" (Gen. 16.10). The purpose of her life is in the promise of the future, not in the painful realities of the present. The angel's promise is Hagar's developing inward certainty, which brings the message that her painful personal existence will evolve into the collective existence of a people.

Only people of sensitive, visionary perception can experience something that transcends their personal world. Only an individual with imagination and an open mind can hear the voice of the angel within, promising the expansion of selfhood into the dimensions of a people. The biblical account attributes these qualities to Hagar, as it does to Abram. Hagar is the only woman to achieve the right of "paternity," although her descendants will become an independent and opposing people. This is a form of negative image, since Hagar is so closely associated with the world of nature and idolatry.

Let us compare the wording of the promise made to Hagar—"I will greatly multiply thy seed, that it shall not be numbered for multitude"—with that of the message given to Abram—"for all the land which thou seest, to thee will I give it, and to thy seed" (Gen. 13.15).

Genesis 17 promises the birth of Isaac: "And I will establish My covenant with [you], for an everlasting covenant, and with [your] seed after [you]" (17.19), whereas the promise concerning Ishmael is: "I will multiply him exceedingly" (17.20). The promise of national greatness that is given to Abraham and Isaac includes the promise of land, the psychic symbol of substance. In contrast, at no point is land promised to Hagar or Ishmael. Without soil and a psychic association with it, Hagar or Ishmael are destined to be wanderers, condemned to doubt and misgivings. They do not enter into a covenant with God. There is neither a bilateral commitment nor any mission assigned to Ishmael ("And he shall be a wild ass of a man; his hand shall be against every man, and every man's hand against him"— Gen. 16.12). Ishmael, the son of Hagar, is not bound by his father's undertaking. He is the son of his mother, who sacrifices her well-being for his sake. Because she gives him herself, he is hers. As a slave, however, she has does not have the right to acquire land. And, because she is an Egyptian and does not belong to Abram's family, she and her son ultimately are expelled from it.

Abram presumably is in the encampment in the midst of this drama; we are not told that he was elsewhere. Yet, his voice is not raised in protest against the wrong being done to Hagar, nor does he regret her flight or express pleasure or any other emotion upon her return. Abram maintains his silence in all matters having to do with Hagar, having declined responsibility for her when he says to Sarai, "Do to her that which is good in thine eyes." His silence reduces his personal stature, and the biblical account makes no attempt to rehabilitate this unflattering image. Abram appears as a man who submits to his wife, who, in turn, rules him with an iron hand and acts as she wishes in her home.

The Sages, realizing that the nation's hero and founder did not measure up to their ethical standards, took care in their *aggadot* to relieve him of the negative attributes so evident in this episode (Bailik and Ravnitzki 1951). In psychological terms, they repressed Abraham's negative side and fashioned a hero-image that satisfied their own ethical imperatives. The virtue of the biblical account is in its rich and varied depiction of Abram. At times he appears strong; at other times, weak. He is human, not an omnipotent mythical hero who is the object of projections.

Abram is eighty-six years old when Hagar bears Ishmael, as stated in the concluding verse of Genesis 16: "And Abram was fourscore and six years old, when Hagar bore Ishmael." Genesis 17 opens thus: "And when Abram was ninety years old and nine, the Lord appeared." The juxtaposition of these verses should not be regarded as coincidental. The biblical account implies that fourteen years passed without a divine revelation. This is quite a long time, and it assumes that Hagar is given to Abram immediately after the revelation in the Covenant of the Pieces. With the birth of Ishmael, Abram fulfills one of his innermost longings—he becomes a father.

Five

The Symbolic Meaning of Names

Since the Covenant of the Pieces the voice has not been heard. There have been no numinous experiences nor any encounters with God.

Clearly, no individual can be constantly under the kind of psychic tension and on the special level of consciousness that permits the frequent recurrence of such encounters with the divinity. Such a long silence, however, is telling. Every encounter with the divinity— the Self—is another stage in Abram's personal psychic development.

Every such encounter brings him one step closer to the climax of his life and his last encounter with God—the binding of Isaac. Every encounter is a milestone in his development through the process of individuation—a process that seems, however, to have come to an abrupt halt, as may be adduced from the lack of biblical evidence of its continuance. We, however, believe that Abram's development has simply assumed a new aspect: the development of his paternal personality, which will have a tremendous impact in the binding of Isaac, his son.

Perhaps the voice of the Self is not heard and does not call him, since he is involved in developing this aspect of his personality primarily by filling it with attributes that are new to him. Being a father (to Ishmael) seems to satisfy his emotional needs, leaving no room for other experiences. Perhaps because the son is Ishmael, the biblical account does not refer to him. Abram has thirteen years to assimilate and come to terms with the experience of fatherhood.

During this period Abram concentrates on looking after his family. He is in the here and now, which is important for his individ-

47

uation process. He is a father, not only a son, as mentioned above. When Ishmael reaches manhood, Abram, enriched by the experience of parenthood, is free and available for new experiences. The divine voice is heard once again. A new command arises from the unconscious: "Walk before Me, and be thou wholehearted" (Gen. 17.1).

The word used in Hebrew, *tamim*, "whole-hearted," means, *inter alia*, "whole." Abram evidently feels he is not "whole" with his God; and, indeed, why would he receive a command unless he were lacking in something? Being a father has diverted Abram's attention from what has thus far been the spiritual focus of his life— the divine presence—to the child and his care. He does not devote himself wholeheartedly to his relationship with the divinity, as required, or, more precisely, according to his understanding of his relationship with God. As the boy grows, no longer needing his father, an inner voice provides a reminder of a person's duty on the path to individuation: "Be whole-hearted"—be whole with yourself and with your God. Abram no longer has room to deviate from the path he chose when he left Mesopotamia. All his psychic resources are directed toward and focused on this goal.

Tamim also means "straightforward, pure, free of any blemish or misdoing"—in both the ethical and physical senses. The demand to be free of any moral blemish, to be upright, is self-evident; it applies to anyone who strives for spiritual integrity and inner truth, and the individual casts it into the form of a religious command arising from that person's image of the divine.

We believe that *tamim* has a physical connotation, as well as that which was expressed later on in the laws of purity regarding the cleanliness of the family and of the body. Tanim also means "naive"; thus the Hebrew imperative may be construed as "Be like a simple child"—credulous, free of doubts, free of questions and vacillations. It means to believe unreservedly, to trust one's father to guide one along a smooth path. Now that Abram has experienced fatherhood and knows the ways of children, he understands what it means for a child to place absolute trust in his father—the kind of trust Abram will be asked to show when God commands him to sacrifice Isaac.

Following the demand that Abram be wholehearted, pure, and straightforward, the promise to keep the covenant between Abram and God is repeated. If the condition "walk before Me and be wholehearted" is met, the covenant between them will remain when

Abram moves to a more significant level in his journey to his Self, as expressed in the change of his name from Abram to Abraham ("Thy name shall be Abraham; for the father of a multitude of nations have I made thee"—Gen. 17.5).

The act of naming a person or an object has magical significance and a meaning that directly affects the personality. In a sense, the act of naming defines the powers that the person acquires as a result of the meaning of his name. This is the origin of the custom of inserting the names of divinities into individuals' names, as in Ezekiel, Jeremiah, and so on.

Naming a person is tantamount to conferring upon them the power implicit in the meaning of the name. When a person acquires a name, they are conferred with vitality, with a soul, with content. The changing of Abram to Abraham has many meanings, the most salient of which is that his new name gives him new strength, new life, and a new personality, as a result of the addition of the letter *h*, which also signifies the name of God. Thus renamed, he is as if reborn. An echo of this process may be found in the custom, prevalent to this day, of giving a seriously ill person, whose life is in danger, the name *Chaim* "life." Conferring upon the unfortunate one the essence of the name is meant to regenerate the vitality required for the sick person to get well. The new name is not, as is conventionally understood, merely a formality, a change of identity meant, as it were, to confuse the Angel of Death. Rather, the name has new attributes, which can modify the personality and destiny of the individual.

The biblical account explains the addition of the letter *h* to Abram's name as an allusion to his future as "the father of a multitude of nations." Thus is his name endowed with the substance of God's promise that he will become a great nation, reinforcing the covenant between them.

There is much homiletic commentary on the addition to Abram's name. In our opinion, however, its essential and most profound meaning is that *h* signifies God, since the Hebrew letter *heh* often serves as an abbreviation for the name of God. Thus God enters Abraham's innermost being—his Self—endowing him with some of his own power and making himself an inseparable part of Abraham's being, the Self. Thus Abraham becomes the living message identified with God. His name becomes the human symbol of

49

the divine command, an official signature, as it were, that God is alive and acting within humanity.

The names of Abraham's sons as well symbolize the need to confer names that convey the message of God's existence within human beings: Ishmael means "God will hear," and Isaac, from the Hebrew root *Z-H-K* (to laugh) describes the absurdity of an elderly couple having a child, as well as the miracle they experienced as a result of their unwavering faith in the truth that emanates from the innermost voice. Although it is laughable to expect a son at such an advanced age, one is nevertheless duty bound to believe the impossible. The command to "be wholehearted" refers to this—to believing in the impossible, like a child who believes what he is told without using logic, which would affirm the implausibility, indeed, impossibility, of an elderly woman having a baby. This is the belief in miracles that belongs to naive faith.

Rashi notes another significant aspect of Abram's name change. The Hebrew *Avram* means "the father [*av*] of Aram," designating Abram's place of origin. and his status as the father of a people, the Aramites. *Abraham*, however, means "the father of a multitude of peoples." In other words, the change is from a name embracing the meaning of one people to a name bearing a collective message, an allusion to a multitude of peoples.

Further allusions and meanings that are helpful in understanding Abraham's personal development in this process of individuation are found in *Midrash Genesis Rabbah* (1951) a compilation of commentaries from various sources dating from the fourth through sixth centuries (see Lech Lecha, 17, 43, 70, 80 with the *Midrash*). "R. Yehoshua ben Korha said that God took from Sarai and gave half to Sarah and half to Abraham. . . . In R. Shimon bar Yohai's name it was said that "once you were [the letter *yod*] in a woman's name and at the end of the letters, now I am putting you [half of the letter *yod*] in a male's name." The Hebrew letter *yod* at the end of Sarai's name, whose numerical value is ten, is divided in half: into two occurrences of *heh*, whose value is five—five to AbraHam, five to SaraH. Thus Sarah's name also changes from a name with a personal meaning—Sarai, "my Sarah, my master"—to a name with a collective meaning—the Sarah of all humankind.

The most profound personal and pan-human interpretation of the changing of Abram's name to Abraham is found in the same section of *Midrash Genesis Rabbah*, which alludes to the solution of a problem we mentioned above: Abram's insensitivity to the women in his life. The "feminine" letter *heh* is added to his name; the numerical value of the *heh* is half that of the *yod*, with which Sarai's name previously ended. *Heh* is considered a feminine symbol because it is so significant and salient within a woman's name that it may be construed as a symbol of the introduction of "feminine" elements into Abraham's psychic makeup—sensitivity, compassion, mercy, and benevolence. Of these, the last (Hebrew, *hesed*) is the kabbalistic embodiment of Abraham, who projects his benevolence upon the world. *Heh* symbolizes wisdom and kingship (*malkhut*), the "feminine" emanations in the kabbalistic tree of the spheres, indicating that the Kabbalists also regarded *heh* as being endowed with feminine meaning. Up to this stage, these traits were not expressed, even though at the time of separation from Lot, Abraham showed magnanimity, but not the love or compassion that belongs to the sphere of the positive anima that allows openness to feelings, as we mentioned above.

After his rebirth, symbolized by his new name, these feminine attributes imbue Abraham's personality with new breadth and new capabilities. He is more sensitive, better able to experience. Abraham's personality blossoms; his horizons are broadened by including the feminine traits. As a result of his encounter with the positive anima, he is capable of experiences to which he was previously unreceptive.

It hardly stands to reason that Abraham, his name expanded by the *heh* and his personality by its significance, would continue to treat Hagar as he did before, with disregard and lack of sensitivity. Certainly she is the mother of his son, yet she has no significance as a person. Evidence for this is found in Genesis 21, where Sarah wishes to cast out Hagar and Ishmael: "And the thing was very grievous in Abraham's sight on account of his son" (v. 11). True, there is no indication that he regrets the forced departure of Hagar. She was a slave who was not regarded as an equal, in contradistinction to the alienation from Hagar, as before, by delivering her to Sarah, to "do with her what seems fit" (Gen. 16.6). Rather, the text implies that Abraham is hurt by Sarah's demand that Ishmael, and his mother with him, be expelled from his home, for thus Sarah wounds the living proof of his creative force, his fatherhood. The emotional tie of a father's love for his son must therefore be broken

51

at her behest. However, Abraham neither decisively rejects Sarah's demand as contrary to his own ethical point of view nor does he make any reference to Hagar.

Abraham has entered a phase of self-determination. His new name appears to represent a new, different man. Thus the promise and the covenant made with Abram must be reiterated and revalidated; and, in fact, the promise that Abraham will beget a great people, settled in the land assured to him, is repeated.

Six

Circumcision

Abraham, however, must recommit himself to God, undertaking to keep the covenant—himself and his offspring—for eternity. This time, the divine command is for a sacrifice, an endorsement sealing the covenant: the commandment of circumcision, "a token of a covenant between Me and you" (Gen. 17.11).

Abraham, whose personality has grown and acquired new characteristics, is now able to sacrifice part of his own flesh and bear a mark attesting to the existence of the covenant with God. This sign in the living flesh is a deep-seated, weighty, and highly significant commitment.

As in every encounter between Abraham and God, the promise is repeated: Abraham will beget a great nation, which will dwell in the land promised to him. This promise should be construed as a symbol of the joining of opposites. The land represents physical and material space; Abraham represents the human and spiritual dimension. This time, however, Abraham's body seems to symbolize the land, and his psyche the divine spirit within him. His body needs a sign of his belonging to God (i.e., to himself). Thus we are given a manifestation of the symbolic integration of body and psyche.

Circumcision was fairly widespread in the ancient world, as it still is in various contemporary societies. As early as the third millennium B.C.E.., it was conventional practice among the Egyptian aristocracy and other peoples of the Near East. The foreskin was customarily removed during puberty rites in tribal societies as a test of strength and a sign of bravery and maturity; those who successfully passed the test were admitted to adult society. The age of circumcision was ordinarily thirteen or thereabout—the age of Ishmael when Abraham removed his foreskin. Ishmael's circumcision may be seen as a social act marking his entrance into adult society in a conspicuously ritualistic ceremony. Ishmael, however, makes no commitment to God. He neither hearkens nor responds to God's commands, nor does he submit to him. Although circumcised, he remains free of burdens and obligations. This is not the case with Isaac, whose circumcision marks the beginning of a tradition of specifically religious, not merely social, significance. In Jewish tradition, circumcision is performed on the eighth day after the birth of the male child, as it was with Isaac. Some recollection of the timing of Ishmael's circumcision as a ritual social act is found, perhaps, in the ceremony of bar mitzvah, the Jewish boy's coming of age at thirteen years. Ishmael's circumcision may also refer to the practice, then prevalent, of circumcision as a symbolic castration for the sake of the Great Mother (Dreifuss 1965). Maybe circumcision refers to cutting the foreskin to shield the infant from the dangers of bad and harmful spirits.

Circumcision represents sexual purification. The removal of the foreskin releases the organ of procreation from all excrescences, which symbolize impurity that must be extirpated. Thus—symbolically—seed is allowed to flow without the impediment of the foreskin. Also symbolically, the removal of the foreskin may be construed as a releasing of the glans, the crown, thereby exposing the source of masculine creation.

Circumcision is deemed necessary for the attainment of spiritual wholeness ("Be thou wholehearted"). By deliberately removing something from the physically whole, by violating the natural integrity of the body, a man symbolically renounces part of his body and his male strength for the sake of the integrity of the spiritual male principle.

In his discussion of sacrifice (1956, par. 671), Jung writes: ". . . a milder form is circumcision. Here at least only a modicum is sacrificed, which amounts to replacing the sacrifice by a symbolical act. By sacrificing these valued objects of desire and possession, the instinctive desire, or libido, is given up in order that it may be regained in new form. Through sacrifice man ransoms himself from his fear of death." Thus men benefit from the sexual energy that is released, reborn, in the act of sacrifice, and human sexuality is elevated to the spiritual domain.

In the *Encyclopedia of Religion and Ethics*, Barton notes that male circumcision among the Semitic tribes originated in sacrifices to a fertility goddess, whose protection was thus solicited for the child, together with blessings and future fertility (Barton 1932, p. 679). Circumcision as we know it today emphasizes not symbolic emasculation but a mutual commitment among men that marks their transition from the family (and parental domination) to the male tribal setting. The result is a fraternity of men that dedicates the foreskin to the male divinity as a sign of the partial sacrifice of physical potency for the sake of the spiritual male procreative principle. This principle, in turn, is invoked for the power it confers on the individual—divine protection and blessings in the form of fertility and male potency.

Circumcision is more than a symbolic act of emasculation and a violation of the body's natural integrity. This sacrifice is significant in terms of a man's stance in relation to nature. An act of this sort, contrary to the pleasure principle and to the integrity and flow of nature, may mark the beginning of human consciousness. Circumcision originates in the need to segregate humanity, previously at one with nature, to set humans apart from the world and its natural laws, and to establish a different set of laws for people as they live within that world. This separation engenders consciousness, education, and independent and autonomous development, because it differentiates people from beasts. In short, the ritual of circumcision means self-control.

The inevitable bloodletting that occurs in this Jewish rite symbolizes spiritual sacrifice ("For the blood is the life"—Deut. 12.23). Life—the psyche—is the spiritual part of the body, and bloodletting, therefore, must be considered a symbolic sacrifice of the psyche. Circumcision thus symbolizes man's total—physical and spiritual—sacrifice.

By offering both facets of himself to the divinity, the circumcised man transcends the sphere of mere corporeal existence and enters that in which his psyche, too, fulfills itself. Only in this fusion of the psychic and physical domains does a man become a man, in a further manifestation of the confluence of opposites—the confluence of body and mind.

The infliction of a blemish, defect, or mark in the flesh is also a symbol of deliberate servitude. The act proclaims the absolute subjugation of the body and the soul to the divinity: a servitude as irrevocable as the physical mark. In the ancient world, this was done to a slave who of his own volition chose to remain in lifelong servitude to his master. In the Bible, Abraham chooses freely, but his descendants do not. They engrave the mark of servitude into their flesh as a manifestation of the undertaking between Abraham and God. Every covenant demands from the participants that they obey and take care of each other.

Circumcision has become a metaphor denoting spiritual and ethical purification. When the prophet Jeremiah exhorts, "Circumcise yourselves to the Lord, and take away the foreskins of your heart" (Jer. 4.4), he in fact is demanding that men escape their psychic indifference, their insensitivity to social or religious evils. Circumcision thus improves and refines a man, giving him the possibility of fulfilling his latent attributes and powers. Furthermore, it is an act of free will, arising from a state of purification. It is a release from domination by instinct (nature), a departure from the sphere of the ego and an ascent to the realm of sensitivity toward others.

The combination of Abraham's name change and the command of circumcision in a single chapter may be the origin of the Jewish tradition of naming the newborn at the circumcision ceremony. An infant on whose body an act contrary to nature has been performed is no longer one of his people; he has been separated from it and set apart as a person in his own right, with his own name. The child is given an identity as an individual, coupled with an automatic collective affiliation as a Jew.

After his circumcision and name change, Abraham is reborn, with a new identity, into a specific collective that is created in purity. He had acquired a nearly superhuman potential, with which he may withstand the ordeals of the future. At the same time, he retains his human image—until the terrible test of the binding of Isaac, in which he nearly departs from the ambit of human beings.

Now that his specific national identity is declared, a nation should be born, but Abraham is a father to Ishmael only; God promises the birth of Isaac. This name is given to a son to be born unnaturally. For a moment, Abraham forgot what he had learned from experiencing God—that there is a paradoxical reality, one with specific rules by which Abraham could act according to the demands arising from the Self—God. Obeying these demands forces him to face and collide with the customs of his society; his set of values is different, strange, and forbidding. Thus, he is alone: the price a man pays for individuation.

The definition of Abraham's personal and collective uniqueness creates a schism between him and his environment. However, only in isolation, in singularity—only when one is alone—can one listen to and hear the voice that emanates from the Self. "And the Lord appeared unto him by the terebinths of Mamre, as he sat in the tent door in the heat of the day" (Gen. 18.1). Here, the biblical account indicates the time and place of the encounter with the divine, manifested in the form of three men. It occurs at midday, when Abraham is seated at the door of his tent.

This posture is significant. The tent door symbolizes Abraham's psychic receptiveness after the experience of his most recent encounter with the divinity. In Jungian terms, an encounter with the divinity is the equivalent of commands and duties arising from the Self, which are performed by the I and the unconscious part of the Self. Abraham has assumed a posture in which he is receptive to the message arising from his Self. Perhaps this sensitivity arises from his name change, which led to a rebirth, as well as the experience of his circumcision, the pain and associated dangers of which have most likely left him disoriented. In this condition he is receptive to the urgent messages of the internal voice. Rashi, quoting R. Hama Ben Hananiah, explains that the words "And the Lord appeared," referring to the third day after Abraham's circumcision, means that the Almighty came to inquire after his health.

That God appears at midday is also significant. "In the heat of the day" the sun is at its apogee. Midday heat, especially in the Middle East, can affect one's wakefulness. Perhaps Abraham dozed off as he sat at the door of his tent, and entered a hypnagogic state. At the same time, his psychic receptiveness increased, as often happens when one is half awake and half asleep. In this state, a different consciousness may emerge—the greater, broader, and clearer consciousness of a great vision. Many cultures symbolize this consciousness of and receptiveness to the divinity by a depiction of the sun at its zenith, generating extreme heat. The blinding light of midday is also a fitting symbol of that other consciousness, Abraham's innermost truth and receptiveness to the divinity, which cannot be considered distinct from the dazzling light it projects upon humanity. Abraham, however, enriches his psyche in the light of consciousness of the existence of the divinity within his Self. In this situation—a hot noontime, blinding light, and a specific state of mind—Abraham's vision turns inward. His inner vision is realized in the form of three men—a God-image and synchronistic event on which inner reality is projected.

As Abraham is immersed in this reflective and receptive state of mind, three men suddenly appear before him—in a form of revelation and realization of a psychic vision. As prescribed by the customs of Eastern peoples, for whom hospitality is a sacred duty, Abraham welcomes the strangers joyfully.

The Hebrew of "And the Lord appeared unto him by the terebinths of Mamre" construes the verb in the singular. In fact, the divine presence materializes in the plural, in the form of three men, because no individual can embody, let alone represent, all aspects of the divine. Three is an archetypal number that expresses both strength and activity. Three is the primary, self-contained, whole, and expanded essence of one. For Abraham, this numinous experience takes the form of three who are one.

The power and the force imbued in the number three are expressed in many theologies. In Christianity, three is the essence of the concept of the divinity. In Judaism, the degrees of emanations, or spheres, in Kabbalah are composed of threes plus one in differing compositions, each sphere being a revelation of the visage of the only One in one of his aspects.

According to Rashi, the Sages also divided the functions of the angels' mission into three: to herald the birth of Isaac, to destroy Sodom and Gomorrah, and to heal Abraham. Furthermore, by citing the number precisely when Abraham is visited by the Almighty—the third day after his circumcision—the Sages attest to its great power and significance. The three men also symbolize collective energy—the energy of the multitude. The augury of the birth of Isaac, the expansion of Abraham's personality to embrace an entire people, must be expressed by collective means—thus, the three.

The hubbub that occurs as Abraham and his entire household place themselves at the guests' disposal is appropriate in an episode in which the birth of Isaac is again proclaimed, with precise indication of the time of the upcoming event. This time the promise is not abstract. The voice of the unconscious is heard because of Abraham's unchallenged inner faith, based on incognizant knowledge, that Sarah will bear him a son "when the season cometh round" (Gen. 18.10). Abraham is receptive to a paradoxical message: that the miracle—a childbirth utterly contrary to the laws of nature—can occur. Such a promise needs threefold reinforcement, which is why three man-angels bring Abraham the news. Sarah, representing Abraham's corporeal side, cannot share his faith.

Sarah, the woman of little faith, symbolizes doubt in miracles; she represents a cold logic, one rooted in knowing the natural laws that rule the world. She does not share Abraham's ability to recognize how miracles may manifest themselves. Though he does express doubt—"And he laughed. . . . Shall a child be born unto him that is a hundred years old?" (Gen. 17.17)—Abraham can conceive differently of the world; in the struggle between natural logic and his belief in a truth that arises from within himself, it is Abraham's belief—his faith—that triumphs.

Sarah, however, represents more than the mere physical aspect of Abraham's being; she also stands for one who dwells in a particular setting and cannot dissociate from it. She is a woman of a certain character. In this part of the biblical account, another aspect of her personality comes to light: denial, spiced with levity, of the angels' message. "Then Sarah denied" expresses, above all, an attempt to avoid consequences, to repress, to negate and nullify an uncomfortable reality.

"And Sarah denied, saying, 'I laughed not'" (Gen. 18.15). She apparently fears the intensity of Abraham's faith, his awesome personality at the moment the divinity is revealed, and his religious fervor. Abraham changes completely when the voice speaks from within. He becomes great and mighty, omnipotent, rigid in his faith. When he undergoes a numinous experience—an encounter with God—he is capable of anything, including the sacrifice of his son and the near-loss of his own human dimension.

There is reason to fear a person in the throes of religious fervor. The intensity and strength of Abraham's faith in his powers release a vast energy in his mind. As the divine image arises from within, Abraham is nearly comparable to the divinity himself.

Seven

Abraham Opposing the Destructive Force of God
and the Problem of the Shadow

The debate between Abraham and the raging God on the issue of Sodom and Gomorrah may be seen as an inner debate between the destructive and the compassionate human elements. Thus far, Abraham has experienced the divinity as One who accompanies him, revealing and distancing himself, but always private and personal, even though God refers to the future multitude of his seed. In the account of the destruction of Sodom and Gomorrah, Abraham's personal divine image is given a further dimension, that of association with a multitude. The divinity wishes to punish a group that has sinned against him—against Abraham's ethical standards, which differ from those of the denizens of Sodom.

Abraham thus becomes a human "ethical yardstick," through which concepts of good and evil are measured for both humanity and God. In contrast to the omnipotent divine image, which embraces the possibility of destruction and annihilation, the human being stands as a symbol of life, an advocate of righteousness and compassion, the divine aspect of the Self in confrontation with the human aspect. In this confrontation, God—the destructive aspect—overcomes the compassionate human side. Abraham's plea for the sparing of Sodom is a manifestation of humanness in confrontation with the destructive, the divine. In the biblical account of Abraham's argument with God, the divine image elevates Abraham to a state of equality, of consultancy ("Shall I hide from Abraham that which I am doing?"—Gen. 18.17), as if the divine image needs a human dimension, which, by penetrating, causes the divine image to mellow and becomes essential and integral within it.

Let us restate our view that Abraham's dialogue with God is in fact a debate within Abraham's psyche, the divine image being an impression and projection of a force at work within the Self. We are not dealing with the nature of the transcendental divinity, of which we know nothing. We simply assume, basing our thought within one weltanschauung or another, that this divinity exists as a manifestation of infinite strength and potential. The divine image is a vast internal power, emanating from within the Self, that acquires substance and makes itself heard according to the needs of the moment. The image of the divine parallels changes in the person; the divine image is by nature dynamic. The human being projects her development, aspirations, and hopes, as well as changes in her intellectual and socio-ethical worldview, onto the divinity and thus modifies its image.

In this instance, Abraham's divine Self ignores the full potency of the destructive forces churning within him against Abraham himself and his actions, passing sentence on a different population: the people of Sodom and Gomorrah. The debate between Abraham and God is, in effect, a form of self-inquiry as to the limits of his ethical jurisdiction and powers of destruction.

Abraham lays down precise and fully defined limits. The first of these is an examination of the facts: "I will go down now and see whether [they have done altogether] according to the cry of it" (Gen. 18.21). This shows that the divine image is not omniscient; it has its deficiencies, like Abraham the man. The second limit is God's assurance that the righteous will not perish with the wicked: "I will not destroy [Sodom] for the sake of ten" (Gen. 18.32). With this we learn a further ethical precept: explicit and unequivocal rejection of collective punishment. The argument also points at the possibility of a change in the verdict, since the divine image is free neither of vacillation nor of uncertainty.

The most vehement criticism of the human versus the divine image, both emanating from the Self, is expressed in Abraham's query: "Wilt Thou indeed sweep away the righteous with the wicked?" (Gen. 18.23). Abraham cannot acquiesce to the possibility that God, in His blind wrath, might annihilate everything in His path, neither considering the righteous nor distinguishing between them and the sinners. In Abraham's opinion, every individual should be punished accordingly.

This ethical struggle between different parts of the psyche simultaneously affects and modifies both the ego and the Self. The ego emerges strengthened by the possibility of an argument that ends with the modification of the divine image arising from the Self. The divine image apparently needs human attributes that reduce and constrain the destructive forces within the psyche. This is the dynamic of change and interrelation between ego and Self, which triggers change in the perception of the divinity throughout the annals of humankind.

Something similar occurs in the dialogue between God and the devil in Job, chapter 1. Abraham's God embraces both good and evil, whereas the divinity in Job is partitioned: the embodiment of good, as it were, plays the human role of Abraham as an advocate of righteousness, while Satan, the destructive side, is the embodiment of evil. In the worldview articulated in Job, the divine image is purged of its destructive attributes, and the entity of Satan is separated and differentiated by characteristics that represent evil. The God-image is separated from its all-embracing image, the embodiment of good and evil alike, and acquires a monovalent dimension as the epitome of good. Thus two powers are created: one representing good—God—and the other embodying evil—Satan.

However, a representative divinity that embraces both good and evil, which accepts the possibility of evil within the godhead, is intolerable in a philosophy that demands steady ethical progress toward the good. Thus the divinity has to be purged of the evil within it. The evil in the world, which cannot be disregarded, is a separate entity that either must be combatted or submitted to. Such evil contests the ruling of the world with the God who represents absolute goodness.

In Job, God neither deprives Satan of the power to exercise evil against Job nor displays overt sensitivity to Job's fate. This laissez-faire approach reflects the dualist philosophy that pervaded the ancient pagan world, whence this story entered the Bible. Some consider the Job account to have originated in Persia, where dualism was accepted. There, so the theory goes, it penetrated certain *aggadot*, in which Satan appears and attempts to prevent the binding of Isaac.

Like God in the Job story, Abraham must harness his positive, creative energy to the negative force that has gained sway over him and threatens to destroy everything in the violent trance that engulfs him. The same process occurs when he hears the command that Isaac be offered up as a sacrifice to God. The role of Abraham as the I is to restore the human dimension to the Self, to become aware of the destructive forces, to segregate them from their constructive counterparts, and to be conscious of the multiple facets of energy imbued in the Self.

The intensity of this energy, which is lacking in ethical judgment, threatens to overwhelm everything in its path. Abraham, representing the ego, has to muster ethical strength and the ability to distinguish between good and evil, and, as his weltanschauung prescribes, to channel this energy into an ethical path. The energy of the Self, in the case of Sodom and Gomorrah, proceeds to judge a collective, punishing an entire populace.

The greatest danger Abraham must avoid is the domination and destruction of the ego by the outpouring of this energy from the Self, for the ego is liable to collapse under the intensity of this energy and be consumed by it. When the Self assumes the ego's place, the personality becomes inflated, driven by instincts devoid of discretion or judgment vis-à-vis the creative and destructive forces; it adopts an indiscriminate, all-embracing attitude. It is the role of the ego—Abraham—to distinguish between these aspects and liberate the Self from this all-embracing posture.

The biblical account implies that God can err. Ten righteous men are not found to set aside the sentence of annihilation passed by the Self on the population of Sodom and Gomorrah. References to human bargaining with the potencies of judgment and destruction are found in folktales the world over. These stories delineate righteous people who manage, by virtue of their human abilities, to rescind harsh sentences passed on the world. Consider "The Devil and Daniel Webster," the village zadik, and many others.

Another way of construing Sodom and Gomorrah is as a symbol of the negative ethical and sexual forces at work in Abraham's psyche. These forces must be extirpated so that the residues of idolatry that the Bible associates with ethical, not only religious, sin may be purged. Sodom and Gomorrah become symbols of perverted sexuality. They are obliterated because ten righteous men other than Lot and his family, by whose virtue they would be spared, cannot be found.

As Genesis 19 indicates, Lot is spared because of his hospitality—he hosts two angels who have come to investigate the "cry of it" and to warn Lot against the wrath of the Almighty about to descend on the "cities of the Plain." Lot's virtue includes his defense of these two men, without regard for the peril involved for himself and his daughters, as he confronts the mob of Sodomites who wish to abuse the two strangers. Interestingly, it is only at the end of Genesis 19 that an ostensibly casual reference to Lot's salvation as a result of his kinship with Abraham is made. Until then, the account describes only Lot's own actions.

Abraham does not plead for the lives of Lot and his family in his negotiations with God. He undoubtedly knows they are living in Sodom; this is stated explicitly in the account of his parting from Lot after the quarrel between the herdsmen ("And Lot dwelt in the cities of the Plain, and pitched his tents, as far as Sodom"—Gen. 13.12). It is also indicated when Abraham rescues Lot and his family, who have been taken captive ("And they took Lot, Abram's brother's son, who dwelt in Sodom, and his goods, and departed"—Gen. 14.12). Why did Abraham fail to plead for his nephew's life at that time? And why, after the destruction of the cities, does Abraham fail to show an interest in the fate of Lot and his family, who fled and took shelter in a cave, without requesting their uncle's assistance?

Evidently the schism between the two families—families of identical background, who left Ur by virtue of the same command ("Get thee out"; heard, it is true, only by Abraham)—is such that they cannot find a common language. Lot, so it seems, simply followed in Abraham's wake.

The inner command that can trigger one person's regeneration may be greeted by another as the continuation of a known way of life—the familiar pattern of the nomad, with no internal message whatsoever. Lot's decision to settle in Sodom—a city with a well-defined tradition, contrasted to Abraham's eternal peregrinations and quests—points to the different internal processes at work in their respective psyches. Abraham may view Lot's settling in Sodom as an act of establishing roots and assimilating into the local population, an act whereby Lot forfeits his singularity and, with it, his psychic "membership" in Abraham's family.

In Sodom, Lot is again surrounded by the world of pagan concepts. His grasp of the new conceptual world evolving in Abraham's tents is erased. His regression is complete. In exchanging one form of paganism for another, Lot returns to a familiar world, to tried and tested concepts that he has known since childhood. Because he is depicted in the biblical account as a man whose personal development contrasts and clashes with Abraham's—a person whom Abraham must contest—Lot may be viewed symbolically as Abraham's repressed counterimage, his shadow.

In various mythologies, the hero, to achieve inner integrity and victory, has to struggle to overcome dangers and obstacles, each of which seems to be a different aspect of his mind. This is so if we view mythologies as early spiritual-psychic creations expressing the primal need to explain various phenomena, within which the heroes' images and actions serve as archetypal symbols. Thus the dangers represented by the people and events experienced by Abraham should be construed as different parts of his psyche, which he must overcome in order to achieve personal perfection and integrity.

According to the biblical account, it is through incest—unwitting, to be sure—that Lot becomes the forefather of the Ammonites and Moabites, who fight the Israelites. Just as Lot represents the shadow side of Abraham on the personal level, on the collective level his descendants represent the shadow side of the people of Israel. The Israelites' repeated regression to idolatry and, concomitantly, to unceasing wars with these nations should be viewed in this context.

Nevertheless, the question remains: why does Abraham, in his argument with God, fail to plead for the lives of Lot and his family? Why does his consciousness obliterate Lot, displaying not even a hint of concern and compassion for the members of his family? Abraham responds to the annihilation of Sodom and Gomorrah with indifference—no other emotion is suggested. He expresses neither grief nor compassion; neither does he celebrate the destruction of evil.

The most likely explanation for this, we believe, is in our explanation of Lot as Abraham's shadow. The elements of the psyche represented by Lot are the most primitive and primeval aspects of Abraham—aspects with which he has yet to come to terms. Had he already done so, he would have felt confident relating to Lot as a human being, instead of as a potential menace that must be repressed lest it overtake him.

Lot's role as Abraham's shadow is the source of Abraham's disinterest in Lot's fate. Such disinterest functions as a defense mechanism that protects Abraham's shaky self-confidence. Lot represents a threat to Abraham's values, which have not yet coalesced into a confident personality. Abraham, still gripped by doubt, cannot relate to Lot, and must therefore refrain from any contact with him.

The account of Lot is rife with sexual inferences, and we must deal with these, as well as with subsequent verses concerning Avimelech and Sarah. Lot is associated with the people of Sodom and Gomorrah, whose sexual predilections are described in some detail in Genesis. By living in their midst, he has acquired some of their uncleanness. Moreover, he is the father of his daughters' sons—he has committed incest. Abraham, too, has transgressed in this domain; we recall that Sarah is his sister. Again, we cannot but regard the sexual problems that accumulate in these two chapters of Genesis as a regression to earlier stages in human existence, before sexuality was enveloped in all kinds of inhibitions and taboos.

Of course, sexuality today is a source of problems and doubts, since human consciousness has not yet come to terms with it, even if we consider ourselves liberated. There is a constant clash between the layers of inhibitions and taboos that are imposed on human sexuality, on the one hand, and the most primeval personality drives, on the other. Humanity has yet to come to proper terms with its repressed sexuality; it has not adequately integrated it into its psyche, which is why it is dangerous. In the typical male-dominated society, woman is the object of sexuality and, as such, a menace. She must not be touched in any way, whether symbolically or in fact. As in early patriarchal societies, women continue to symbolize the threat to male domination and supremacy. Despite major changes in society and women's role in it, these attitudes have survived. After millennia of inhibitions and taboos, sex and sexual activity are still suspect.

Were the human sex instinct integrated into the monotheistic weltanschauung, the procreation-based worldview would naturally be projected onto the divine image as well. True, the biblical account states, "In the image of God created He him; male and female created He them" (Gen. 1.27). The divine image, however, is regarded as endowed with masculine attributes only. The divine image is never called "she." Women's role in the procreative process is symbolically fulfilled by the earth, from which, monotheism states, the first human was created. In contrast, the pagan world speaks of the procreative coupling of a god and goddess endowed with male and female characteristics, as in nature.

Had men, raised in a world marked by monotheism, come to terms with the sexual impulse, they would not have needed to create the myth of the virgin birth, on the one hand, and prohibitions against contact with women, on the other. Perhaps such confusion about sexuality is why Lot's wife had to be turned into a pillar of salt: Lot had to be in a position to experience incest, descend to the most primitive psychic stratum—a total regression to the pagan world, to nondifferentiated, uninhibited sexuality, to primordial instinctivism. In this fashion, Abraham is released from his shadow, Lot.

Regression does not bear a negative connotation if it belongs to a developmental process that signals change. Ups and downs, retreats and advances, are requisite parts of the process. It is possible that Abraham's indifference to Lot and to the fate of his family belongs to the stage of regression in which Abraham finds himself. The same may be said about the episode concerning Sarah and Avimelech. Abraham's marriage to his sister, his dissembling about his relationship with her, and his problems in dealing with her actions all belong to this stage.

Why does Abraham lie to Avimelech and introduce Sarah as his sister? ("She is my sister . . . and he took Sarah"—Gen. 20.2.) Only one explanation suggests itself: he remembers his previous experience with Pharaoh. Genesis 12.12 states explicitly: "And the Egyptians will see you and say: This is his wife; and they will kill me, but you they will keep alive." However, in the case of Avimelech, king of Gerar, nothing is said that forces Abraham to lie in order to save his life.

Fear, another attribute of regression, prevents Abraham from properly judging his neighbors. At this stage, Abraham does not discern the difference between Pharaoh and Avimelech. The major difference is strikingly illustrated by the meaning of the latter's name— "father-king." Whereas *Pharaoh* is a specifically Egyptian expression and title, *Avimelech* indicates a status, title, and Semitic origin close to that of Abraham, who may therefore expect him to behave in a manner close to his own, one comprehensible to him. Severely intimidated, however, Abraham cannot make this distinction. All ethical considerations are pushed into a dark corner of his psyche, as he considers his life imperiled. Thus, a lie is mobilized in the service of life.

This is a situation in which Abraham's shadow may gain domination over him. The shadow—one's dark, repressed side, which is negative as long as it remains repressed—serves the existential instinct of survival. There is no unalloyed and unequivocal yardstick for it. The shadow acquires its negative significance as the manifestation of everything known as "evil" because it is unresolved and repressed, in conflict with one's conscious ethical stance. When it is illuminated by consciousness—when it surfaces and is examined by the conscious mind—the light of understanding is cast upon it and the shadow, as a real shadow, disappears. Accordingly, all negative ethical assertions with regard to the shadow are indefensible, except when the shadow is repressed.

Recognition of the existence of evil, as defined by declared, conscious ethical yardsticks—within the psyche and as an inseparable part of human nature, as an allusion to and a residue of the primitive mind that is so real within people—releases the pressure and potency caused by repression. Recognition of the shadow as a relative and varying essence within the human psyche averts the detonation of this energy via its redirection onto neurotic paths.

Abraham is dominated by the shadow and dissembles. Sarah is then taken to Avimelech's house. Sarah symbolizes Abraham's property in both the material sense and in his mind (the anima)—in the symbolic, psychological realm as the feminine principle within the male psyche. Because Abraham is dominated by his shadow, he forfeits Sarah, part of his real and psychological property.

By acquiring these, Avimelech then becomes a servant of the negative psychic forces—Abraham's, in this case. The biblical account endows Avimlech with unconscious awareness of the sin he is about to commit, according to his own inner criteria and the collective within which he lives. It permeates his consciousness in a dream, warning him of the danger ("But God came to Avimelech in a dream of the night"—Gen. 20.3). Pharaoh, of course, had no such dream.

Only a few individuals in the Bible have prophetic dreams. Those who do are major players, and their influence on events endows their actions with exceptional significance. Hence the great importance of Avimelech's dream in this context, not only because of the sin he nearly commits after being misled by Abraham, but also because of the significance he acquires by having had the dream. Avimelech therefore must be viewed as the pagan portion of Abraham's psyche, with which he is struggling.

Dreams, says Jung, are neither volitional human creations nor arbitrary events. Dreams are fashioned from the innermost substance of one's psyche, substance of which one is unaware and which surfaces only when one sleeps. Jung comments:

> Therefore the dream is, properly speaking, a highly objective, natural part of the psyche, from which we might expect indications, or at least hints, about certain basic trends in the psychic process. Now, since the psychic process, like any other life process, is not just a causal sequence, but is also a process with a teleological orientation, we might expect dreams to give us certain indicia about the objective causality as well as about the objective tendencies, . . . (1953, par. 210)

Avimelech's "objective evidence" is the unconscious knowledge that Sarah is forbidden to him. Avimelech accuses Abraham of almost leading him to sin, and he rightly demands an explanation. Abraham's response—"She is indeed my sister, the daughter of my father, but not the daughter of my mother" (Gen. 20.12)—requires deep psychological inquiry, deeper than Rashi provides: "It was the custom among heathens to marry their sisters and, having so married, they were still heathens." This practice did indeed exist among the peoples of the region. But the marriage between Abraham and Sarah is not incestuous in the conventional sense, and so is not prohibited under Jewish and gentile law. It should be viewed rather as the prerogative of heroes and gods only, who, as symbols and archetypal representatives of forces within the psyche, are not bound by human constraints. Here Abraham has transcended the bounds of conventional human laws. Later he is able, in the episode of the binding of Isaac, to step outside the realm of humankind and its emotive commands, almost sacrificing his son to the Almighty.

As Abraham's sister, the image of Sarah bears additional significance, which warrants consideration. When friendly to the ego, the anima—the set of ostensibly feminine attributes deeply embedded in the male psyche—endows a man with a receptiveness to the world of feelings, senses, and intuition, from which he derives his creative ability and openness to the world beyond the rational: the transpersonal-transcendental essence with which Abraham is graced.

As a component of the male psyche, the anima comprises symbols of feminine images, of which the most salient are mother and sister. The sister-image is characterized by devotion, willingness to sacrifice herself, and unconditional love, providing a man with succor and support. Note here that in our culture *Sister* has traditionally referred to women who nurse, alleviate suffering, provide support and assistance, and tend to the needs of others, or who love and protect, as in Chaim Nachman Bialik's famous poem "And Be Thou to Me a Mother and a Sister." In the biblical account as well, Sarah comes to Abraham's aid, clutching his life and well-being in her hand.

The problem with the anima is that male society considers "feminine" characteristics ill-suited to the ordinary man, who therefore represses them. Thus, many parts of the anima are almost always left in the unconscious, where, like any repressed element of the psyche, they accumulate an energy that is not freely expressed and therefore assumes a negative character. Perhaps Abraham must tell Avimelech, frankly and with full awareness, that "She is my sister." Perhaps this is the only way he may become aware of the projection of his anima on Sarah, so as to release the energy that has acquired negative attributes—the energy that has crossed over to the shadowy side—in order to redirect it along positive lines.

At this point we should explain the mechanism of projection, about which Jung states: "But anything that exceeds the bounds of a man's personal consciousness remains unconscious and therefore appears in projection." (1956, par. 507). Elsewhere, Jung explains:

> Nature, the object par excellence, reflects all those contents of the unconscious, which, as such, are not conscious to us. Many nuances of pleasure and pain are perceived by the senses as unthinkingly attributed to the object, without our pausing to consider how far the object can be made responsible for them. (1956, par. 170, n. 84)

Furthermore, the mechanism of projection does not operate in a vacuum. The person who projects needs an object—nature, as indicated, or some event or human image endowed with characteristics that agree to cooperate, as it were, with the projector. In other words, the very essence of one who receives the projection must provide some indication of the content of the material being projected.

The path of individuation is the elimination of projections, including the acceptance of ostensibly nonmasculine traits within the psyche as essential elements of the personality rather than as masculine weakness. Only when Abraham individuates can Sarah live independently as a flesh-and-blood human being, rather than as an object of psychological projections, or as a symbol. In this way, she is freed to fulfill her autonomous task and may bear a son.

Expressed otherwise, Abraham projects his unconscious psychic images—the anima—onto Sarah, who receives Abraham's projections either wittingly or unwittingly, without checking them, without investigating them, and without elucidating for herself the extent to which his projections—the psychic attributes he has ascribed to her—actually coincide with her real attributes. In this fashion she plays into his hands, allowing him to use her as a target for his projections.

Thus, it is not only Avimelech who views Sarah as a sexual object: so do the shadow parts of Abraham's psyche, as represented by Avimelech. In his struggle with his shadow, Abraham achieves an awareness of Sarah's personal autonomy. Avimelech changes from a hostile and threatening shadow to one that serves the process of Abraham's individuation.

When a person is freed of stress and projections, he gains access to the psychic energy that has previously been repressed. Hence the compensation given Abraham by Avimelech—the cattle and slaves, male and female, symbols of power and status that, logically, Abraham should give Avimelech for avoiding wrongdoing— may be seen as the enrichment of psychic energy. It is therefore perfectly natural that Avimelech, formerly Abraham's shadow, is the one to confer gifts, which symbolize the psychic reinforcement and positive, constructive energy released by Abraham's new understanding of Sarah's status within his psyche.

Eight

Sarah, Abraham, and the Shadow

Jung's definition of the anima as the archetype of life coincides with the Jewish view of Sarah as the fountain of life of the people of Israel, the mother of the collective. "And the Lord remembered Sarah."

Isaac is born as promised and is subjected to the commands of membership in the people of Israel. Isaac is born into a group defined in national-religious terms. He does not have the right—given to Abraham—to choose how he will define himself. He is his father's son. He is alive because he is the successor to his father—one who inquired and demanded, sought and clarified possibilities, took a decision, and made a choice. His life is given him by Abraham, as is his possible death.

"And Abraham was a hundred years old when his son Isaac was born unto him" (Gen. 21.5). Abraham's age at Isaac's birth is mentioned in part to emphasize the possibility of a miracle, wherein a son is born to an elderly couple as promised them by the Almighty. Abraham's age also has symbolic content, however. All myths, as creations of a society in the course of its development, contain symbols of and allusions to an archetypal essence—an essence to which the narrators belong and which is considered as having magic substance and effect.

The number one hundred, the product of ten multiplied by ten, is considered a perfect number. In kabbalistic tradition, the command "Get thee out," which leads Abraham onto the path of individuation that reaches one of its climaxes with the birth of a son and an heir, also contains the value of one hundred; the numerical values of the Hebrew words are thirty, twenty, thirty, and twenty. Thus Abraham's age emphasizes his integrity, as if the birth of Isaac causes him to attain the personal perfection alluded to in the command with which he embarked on his path and which indicates the direction he is to go.

In another approach, the number ten signifies the one divinity, and zero the world that begins and ends at the same place, like the uroboros. The mythical serpent with its tail in its mouth symbolizes beginning and end as the inseparable unity of creation and death—the constant renewal of unconscious and undefined nature—of integrity and unity in infinite dynamism. The numeral one, representing the divinity, is the symbol of the male, the organ of virility. The zero, in its resemblance to the female sexual organ, is a symbol of the feminine. Only when they are combined (as in copulation) do they express the forces that create the whole. The zero alone is meaningless without the one.

The Hebrew Encyclopedia (1957, vol. 27, p. 804) makes the following comment about the Pythagoreans, the fifth-century B.C.E. Greek sect with a religious philosophy based on numbers:

> The Pythagoreans considered the number 10 to be perfect because it is the sum of 1, 2, 3, and 4, by arraying the points of a triangle. The first unit, from which the world was made, was considered a point tending to an infinite void. Its division or flow created a line defined by points—the territorial instinct (three points) and the surface, the body.

This philosophy was subsequently developed by Aristotle into the individual and the pair, the one and the many, right and left, male and female.

Pythagorean number theory apparently found its way into the neo-Platonic approach and from there into the worldview of Kabbala, which considers ten a symbol of perfection, expressed in the identification of ten spheres through which the divine essence emanates into the world. The ten spheres are largely ordered in sets of three.

The triangle may therefore be viewed as a symbol of sanctity or sanctification. It is possible that the heifer and the ram offered by Abraham during the Covenant of the Pieces (Gen. 15.9) were marked with triangles; the word in 15.9 that supports this theory, *meshulash*, is ordinarily translated as referring to the age of the heifer and the ram—"of three years old," but might also refer to such markings. The triangle may also represent the female pubes, thus symbolizing sexual fertility. We find grounds for this in a figurine of Apis, the Egyptian bull deity, dating from the fifth to eighth century B.C.E. (on display at the Rockefeller Museum in Jerusalem). The figurine has a triangle on its forehead, like the head of a clay bullock or cow from the same period that was discovered in the excavations at the temple of Kitu-mana in the Negev (at the Israel Museum).

Abraham is one hundred years old when Isaac is born. Abraham is whole, or, more precisely, is made whole by the birth of his son. Unlike the birth of Ishmael, where it is stated only that Abraham was eighty-six years old, Abraham's past and future merge into the present of the birth of Isaac.

Sarah is ninety when Isaac is born. Her reactions reveal further aspects of her personality. She does not display the joy of one for whom a miracle has been performed; she does not express gratitude and humility in view of the wonder visited upon her. Rather, she is afraid she will be ridiculed: "God hath made laughter for me; every one that heareth will laugh on account of me." (Gen. 21.6). This is another reason why her son is called Isaac (from the Hebrew root "to laugh"). The Sarah we read about in this verse behaves as a woman who finds it difficult to behave as an ordinary mother; she behaves above all as a woman whose dignity has been offended. The association of this verse with her stay in Avimelech's palace disturbed the Sages, who feared for Sarah's honor, lest it be suspected that she became pregnant in Avimelech's palace. Hence they "delivered" an infant whose face and form resemble Abraham's, so that any suspicion concerning the miracle baby would be nipped in the bud.

Sarah displays no maternal feelings, perhaps because of the many difficulties she has experienced, which over the years drained the reservoir of emotion in the constant battle to maintain her position as the family's "first lady." Perhaps her feelings have simply dulled in her old age. Or maybe it is that the dream of so many years, when finally realized, has emptied her heart. All these are attempts to explain and excuse her reaction upon the birth of her son: "Every one that heareth will laugh on account of me."

Whatever the reasons, Sarah's response is not one of unalloyed joy, as might be expected of a woman who has given birth against all odds.

Moreover, motherhood generally brings an increase in love and compassion, generosity and kindness. But Sarah is true to her tough nature. Being a mother does not soften her heart; the love we assume she has for her newborn does not extend to the people around her. The Sages enhanced and improved on the biblical Sarah when they commented that the phrase "that Sarah should give children suck" (Gen. 21.7) means that she had such an abundance of milk that she could suckle more children. The biblical account, however, shows that she jealously—cruelly—reserves her milk for her own son alone. Similarly, she demands that Ishmael and Hagar be expelled, lest Ishmael share the inheritance with her son ("Cast out this bondswoman and her son; for the son of this bondswoman shall not be heir with my son, even with Isaac"—Gen. 21.10). Sarah is so hostile toward Hagar that she cannot pronounce her name, referring to her instead as "this." By avoiding using Hagar's name, Sarah expresses unbounded contempt for the woman and her son, who are not privileged to have a name. Sarah forgets nothing, bearing her grudges and jealousy forever.

Sarah demands that Hagar and Ishmael be cast out on the pretext that she has seen Ishmael "making sport." Rashi interprets this as "worshipping pagan gods." But how could idolatry exist within Abraham's family setting? Perhaps it was still practiced among the male and female servants and was tolerated by Abraham. If so, however, why is it only Ishmael who is asked to pay the price of withdrawal to the world of his mother and her gods? Perhaps Sarah, in her jealousy, knows that Abraham is willing to forfeit his firstborn, because he has a substitute in her son.

Thus she spurns the child who has lived in her home for thirteen years. Because she views him as a danger to her son, he must be expelled. With no remorse, with the cold calculation of arithmetic gain, she is prepared to send Hagar and Ishmael to certain death in the desert. In fact, this may be just what she wants: to exact revenge on the handmaiden who has played such an active role in Abraham's life—a role that Sarah believes belongs to her alone—as well as on the son who was born as a result of this engagement.

This time, however, in contrast to his earlier evasion of responsibility for Hagar ("Do to her that which is good in thine eyes"— Gen. 16.6), Abraham does not submit meekly to Sarah. His innermost being rebels against the iniquity she demands of him ("And the thing was very grievous in Abraham's eyes on account of his son"— Gen. 21.11). He rejects the demand because it is wholly contrary to his worldview. Moreover, it deviates from the practice by which the sons of handmaidens were considered semilegal or fully legal sons, as in the case of Jacob's handmaidens. It also violates his internal ethical code. Abraham is unable to deny his love for his elder son. Even if this is not stated explicitly, it must be assumed that he loves Ishmael as the first and only fruit of his loins for thirteen years. It also may be presumed that he feels responsibility for the fate of the boy and his mother.

Abraham has an immensely difficult conflict, between submission to the human ethical command and submission to the command of the Self. He must either commit human "evil" or comply with the divine plan in service of the Self.

"And God said unto Abraham. . . . In all that Sarah saith to thee, hearken unto her voice" (Gen. 21.12). The innermost voice guides Abraham when he accedes to Sarah's demand that Hagar and Ishmael be cast out. Sarah, as one of the images of Abraham's anima, unconsciously knows what Abraham must do in his process of individuation, actions that he himself cannot know, since the anima—"Sarah," anchored in his unconscious and thus perhaps repressed toward the side of the shadow, the dark side of his mind—is in the service of the Almighty. It is through her that his mind must develop, even if he—and we—view her as negative in the extreme. (Compare this with the role Eve plays in promoting Adam's awareness, as advised by the serpent, the symbol of darkness, negativity, and shadow; observe Rebecca's behavior in the theft of Isaac's blessing for Jacob, and so on.)

The function of Sarah's demands as the voice of Abraham's anima is to ready him psychically to recognize the existence of the shadow in his psyche, and to accept it consciously. Thus he is prepared for the possibility of the departure and death of his other son, which will occur during the Binding. No ethical consideration applies here. As the anima, Sarah must serve the process of Abraham's individuation; she is a tool in the service of the Self, which demands an action contrary to all of Abraham's ethical precepts and personal criteria. The purposes of the Self go beyond ethical considerations, beyond any determination of good and evil, and the role of the anima is to serve the historical developmental needs of the Self beyond sociocultural conventions. The woman, Sarah, is closer to and sensitive to the unknown. She symbolizes the unconscious. Through the contact with the anima, a man comes into contact with the Self.

The Self—the innermost voice—demands compliance with the voice of the flesh-and-blood woman. Sarah intuitively demands what the Self demands of Abraham's ego. Hagar and Ishmael are sent to the wilderness, out of the house of Abraham, away from his protection and patronage, into the emptiness of the desert. Abraham experiences for the first time what he will experience later with his second son: the pain of dispatching him to possible death. Abraham experiences bereavement and loss of love, so that he may understand that despite the strength of the emotions of frustration, rage, and pain, his life can continue even without the physical presence of Ishmael at his side. Internalizing Ishmael's image and integrating it into his psyche allows Abraham to carry on, overwhelmed as he is by pain, scared and enlarged by his experiences.

In *Depth Psychology and a New Ethics* (1969), Erich Neumann states that the individual must at times obey the shadow—evil—if the Self is to be realized. One must be ready to undertake actions that may be defined as antiethical or nonethical, as in the binding of Isaac. Conventional human ethics are suspended, as Kierkegaard stated. Our here-and-now judgment cannot cope with actions that run counter to our ethical outlook. One might deduce from this that the divine ethic is not necessarily identical to its human counterpart, and that it has goals beyond the ethical considerations accepted by human beings.

Sarah proposes; Abraham disposes. His self-confidence is shaken and he is helpless in dealing with her. Some "external" intervention is required: the voice of God, commanding him to submit to her. The decision is not his; it is transferred to a higher authority. God demands his compliance with the voice of Sarah. It is not his personal decision, but a higher command. Abraham gives up his love and compassion for Ishmael and Hagar, submits to a higher judgment, acts outside of a humane and moral consideration, and sacrifices his son to the desert.

Abraham sacrifices his sons in an ascending order of pain: from the son of the handmaiden to the son of the "first lady" herself. This is a leave-taking from one degree of psychic anguish to another deeper and more painful one. Of Abraham's two sons, only one will remain. First he sacrifices Ishmael, and soon he will sacrifice Isaac—in an infinitely crueler action: the Binding on the altar, a ritual slaughter. In the first sacrifice, the "guilt" is Sarah's, since the divine voice speaks through her. In the second sacrifice, however, the divine voice ordering the action is the voice of the Self, Abraham's internal voice. The sons are sacrificed in a command of sublime origin, one that humans cannot grasp. It is the demand of the Self, which does not take account of the ego (and even acts against it) for the sake of a higher purpose toward which it strives, and which it must achieve, even if this ostensibly nullifies and destroys the ego.

"And Abraham rose early in the morning and took bread and a bottle of water . . . and sent her away" (Gen. 21.14). Abraham sends Hagar and Ishmael away in public view, in the light of the morning. This symbolizes his awareness of the nature of his action and of the need to assuage his conscience by providing them with bread and water for their journey. Naturally, such provisions do not suffice when emotional nourishment is withheld. Hagar and Ishmael have been denied protection and refuge, without which they are condemned to death.

Again, perhaps to keep her death and the death of her son from resting like a blemish, an ethical defect, on Abraham's shoulders, Hagar hears the voice of God promising her present and future life, as well as divine protection for Abraham's future descendants through Ishmael. As in many myths, the rival brothers must continue to exist—they are, after all, of the same origin—each fighting and complementing the other, one symbolizing the hero and the other his shadow. In the ancient world, human understanding was unable to digest the existence of object and anti-object within a single image or essence, and so the separate brothers were created. People needed to draw an unequivocal distinction between good and evil, judging each as best they understood them, basing their judgment on the criteria available to them. It is extremely difficult, even today, to accept the coexistence of "good" and "bad" within a single body. The mythical hero, however, must defeat his shadow and recognize the reality of its existence within him—that it is not an external substance onto which his shadow is projected.

This struggle is the path of individuation. Like all processes, it is composed of ups and downs, retreats and advances. Like any human process, it is never fully achieved because of the limits of the human ability to absorb and perceive.

Thus Ishmael and Hagar, driven away from Abraham's household, withdraw to the pagan world—a world defined as "evil" in the national consciousness of the Jewish people since time immemorial—even though God protects them there. The statement "And his mother took him a wife out of the land of Egypt" (Gen. 21.21) seems to close the circle of Hagar and Ishmael's ordeals and the Egypt-identified "evil" that dominates them. Her selecting an Egyptian spouse for her son returns Hagar's offspring to her own origins, and so Abraham's obligations to her are effectively annulled.

Nine

The Binding

We now come to the binding of Isaac, the most overwhelming and controversial episode in the national religious myth of Judaism. The account begins in Genesis 22: "And it came to pass after these things, that God did prove Abraham." The use of this sentence dealing with God's proving, or trying of, Abraham, testing the extent of his belief in him and his submission to his commands, seems to neutralize the significance of the sacrifice demanded of him at the Binding. Since the biblical account states that God's demand of Abraham is merely a trial and that God does not intend to permit human sacrifice on his altar, the account is stripped of its cruel and necessary substance—if Abraham is to be conceived as the symbol of total belief and the story as an experience which takes the man outside the human boundary to the limits of divinity. In other words, the ego is dominated by the Self and its demands.

Abraham's human personality is nullified as the ego submits to the demands of the Self, the divinity. It is our opinion that the above-mentioned verse was added to the biblical account in a later period, when human sacrifice, not as a practice still prevalent among peoples of the area but in terms of an utterly different ethical worldview, was rejected. This reminds us of the opening of the book of Job, where God and Satan discuss what Job's faith in God would be if he were to be deprived of his goods, wealth, and loved ones. However, since the verse is in the biblical account, it seems to us that in order not to reduce the significance of the Binding as the most terrible human ordeal in an individual's life, the "proving" or "trial" should be construed neither as a trial, nor, as the Sages sug-

81

gest, as an allusion to a miracle, but as the acquisition of experience. (The Hebrew *nisayon*—"experience, test"—stems from the root *N-S-H* "to try.") Such a trial is a person's ordeal when facing an ambivalent God, and it includes some recognition of God's nature.

Nisayon means choosing among the various possibilities that exist in changing situations. It entails clarifying by comparing and contrasting—a cognitive action that involves all the senses and the intellect, which is able to investigate, compare, and deduce. *Nisayon* can also be interpreted as "temptation," a roundabout way of verifying certain assumptions.

When does such a trial take place if the outcome is uncertain, as in Job? It takes place when some fact must be proved or disproved. Thus, such a trial entails doubt, hesitation, or uncertainty as well as disbelief in a given reality or assumption. These attributes make it possible to hold the trial, but they conflict with the possibility of blind faith, in which the kind of absolute sacrifice, such as that demanded of Abraham, may be made. Such faith is the negation of the ego before the Self; for a person of faith, it may even mean sacrificing the body, on the altar of faith and the soul, in order to sanctify the Almighty (*Kiddush ha-Shem*).

In contrast to a "trial" (*nisayon*), the "gaining of experience" (*hitnasut*) means experiencing something without being able to choose from among various possibilities. Abraham has no option other than to experience the encounter with God, as he has before. This time, however, God displays his aggressive side. Abraham's experiencing of the divinity must be whole, and he must therefore encounter an ambivalent God in all his aspects, containing all his possibilities. Abraham can explore neither the nature of the divinity nor the intensity of the experience the encounter entails. The acquisition of experience transcends ethical considerations. It is the experiencing of a psychic or other event that arouses feelings of excitement, agitation, and identification—whether positive or negative—in the absence of any logic or reflection. Neither an ethical yardstick nor any value distinction other than its scale of intensity can be applied.

A posteriori, individuals understand the experiences they have undergone. They assess them, analyze them, and draw conclusions from them on the basis of the means available. In this way they become conscious.

Thus it seems that God, the Self, wants Abraham to undergo

this awesome "test" in order to grow, to gain strength, to transcend the bounds of human experience, and to enter the area of suprahuman experiences. According to both contemporary ethical criteria and those of the period in which the biblical account was committed to writing, a father who kills his son for whatever reason has violated straightforward human limits. From our contemporary perspective, he has ventured into the domain of archaic culture (primitive religion) or suprahuman divine spheres. However, as we have noted, the heroes of myths are presented as being beyond the human dimension, as archetypes symbolizing the paths of human development, containing the entire spectrum of human possibilities. One of these possibilities is a struggle for a position of power. In this struggle, a youngster threatens the domination of an older man and the latter tries to destroy him.

The meaning of the Hebrew *try* means bringing a particular experience upon Abraham. However, since the divinity is omniscient, embracing all, he should know that Abraham will act as required of him, even if his humanity protests. God therefore has no need to actually try Abraham, unless God needs to put himself (as the Self, part of Abraham's personality) on trial. Thus we may conclude that there is an overlapping between God and Abraham (when the ego is conscious of the Self and a dialogue between the two occurs).

Together with this recognition of Abraham's near-divinity—cognizance of the existence of the divine voice within him—it is clear to us that he must ascend to Mount Moriah. He has no other option, for he would be negating himself. If he refuses, he will have negated everything he has done thus far. He will have severed the link between the ego and the Self, and his entire life, which has proceeded according to the orders of the Self, will be rendered meaningless, his actions based on faulty foundations. He therefore cannot violate the divine command, neither by doing away with himself (his life being not worth living) nor by killing his son (killing his love and his future life).

The prima facie significance of the demand to kill his son appears to be a regression to the pagan world of human sacrifice. Infanticide, the sacrifice of the fruit of the womb, was performed in order to compensate and appease the deity so that it would protect the household and increase its fertility.

"And He said to him, 'Abraham,' and he said, 'Here am I.'"

Rashi interprets Abraham's response as signifying submission and meekness. Indeed, the inner voice, the divine command, thus far has acceded to all of Abraham's requests. Because Abraham's experiences with God have been positive, he has no reason to suspect that he is expressing his willingness to commit the most terrible act of his life. He places himself at the service of the divinity with no hesitation, suspicion, or misgivings. Abraham pledges himself to the service of his Lord, who takes on a form completely different from the one he has known so far.

The God who commanded "Get thee out" (to new life) is the same God who issues the command of death. By ordering the Binding, the divinity displays its ambivalence. The God who brings life into being now commands death. The God whose injunctions have been those with which Abraham has been able to cope is now commanding the inhuman, so that Abraham may contend with the human sides of his psyche and transcend the human sphere.

Thrice Abraham replies, "Here am I." The triple repetition indicates the intensity and strength embodied in the form to which Abraham replies, a form containing the obvious as well as the hidden meaning of facing the commanding voice. First, God calls on Abraham to listen to His voice, and he reports to the deity, ready and willing to serve him. The second time is when Isaac turns to him ("And he said, 'My father,' and he said, 'Here am I, my son' . . . 'But where is the lamb for a burnt-offering?'"—Gen. 22.7). The third time is when the angel intervenes to prevent the slaughter ("And the angel of the Lord called upon him. . . . and he said, 'Here am I'"—Gen. 22.11). Abraham is willing to submit to all three demands: to serve God, despite the inhuman demand made of him; to renounce his love for Isaac and commit filicide for the sake of God; and to submit to the merciful aspect of God, who rescinds the initial cruel demand. "Here am I" represents an acknowledgment of the paradoxical multiplicity of the aspects of the divinity, and Abraham's ability to renounce his own humanity to the commands of the Self.

Contrary to convention, the angel is not an emissary of the divinity, a kind of spiritual creation in the service of the Lord, acting according to His will as His emissary to humankind. Here, the angel is another name for the divinity itself, when "the Angel of the Lord" appears before Hagar (Gen. 16.7-14), who "called the name of the Lord that spoke unto her" (16.13). We may deduce that the presence that spoke to her first is identical with the Lord. In Genesis 21.17, by contrast, Hagar and Ishmael encounter the angel of God in the wilderness of Beersheba, where God may hear the voice of the lad. In this instance, the angel of God speaks to Hagar as an emissary of the deity who hears Ishmael's weeping. In these two instances, "the angel of the Lord" bears a message of redemption and life. This angel therefore may be construed as a manifestation of the compassionate aspect of God, who is a unitary divinity with multiple facets.

The Sages, however, had no doubt that the angel of the Lord was a distinct being, God's emissary only. One of the *aggadot* relates that when the angel of the Lord ordered Abraham to halt the sacrifice, Abraham demanded that God Himself issue the command. The lips that issued the interdiction, he argued, are the lips that should rescind it ("He Himself told me and now, if He so requests, let Him tell me"—Bialik and Ravnitzki 1951, Ma'asei Avot 44).

Let us return to Genesis 22.1, with which the episode of the Binding begins: "And it came to pass after these things." The question arises: After what things? Perhaps it was merely the conclusion of the pact with Avimelech as related in Genesis 21, after which the events in Genesis 22 occurred. The Sages, however, could not accept the account of the Binding verbatim, because it was contrary to either their perception of the divinity or of the divine essence as the epitome of good. They therefore focused on this sentence and established a parallel between it and the beginning of Job, the debate between God and Satan. Rather than perceiving the divinity as an ambivalent essence divorced from the assessment of good and evil by the criteria of human ethics, the Sages projected upon God the moral criteria of their world. Satan is the screen onto which evil is projected, and he is responsible for actions that fail to correspond to God's goodness. The expression "and after" seems to allude to the previous debate between God and Satan, in which the latter is empowered to try to tempt Job and Abraham.

Rashi presents the Sages' construction of "and after" thus: "Many of our Sages say: after Satan's provocative statement; namely, from the entire feast Abraham held [on the day Isaac was weaned] he sacrificed to You neither a single bullock nor a single ram. [The Almighty] said to him: But he did it all for his son; had I told him to sacrifice his son to Me, he would not have hesitated" (Rashi *Pentateuch*). Thus Satan is responsible for God's demand that Isaac be sacrificed. God remains "clean"; Satan is responsible for this cruelest of demands. Satan is the embodiment of doubt, so his role is to arouse doubt.

Thus the "evil" in this account is doubt, contrasted to innocent belief, which is "good." Doubt destroys peace of mind, ruptures trust, and causes disquietude concerning God. It is God's intention to test or prove Abraham's belief in him. Satan here is not the personification of "evil," in the sense that he acts as the emissary of evil. Rather, he triggers the attribute of "evil"—doubt—in others who, contrary to their natural attributes, act under its stimulus. Thus Satan challenges the veracity of Abraham's submission and allegiance to God.

It is as if Abraham has forgotten and neglected God. His earthly love for Isaac disrupts the harmony that had reigned between him and God, as love can disrupt the order of things. Abraham's long-awaited fatherhood fills his entire being. He is utterly caught up in Isaac, as may be inferred from the long silence in communication between God and Abraham following the birth of Ishmael. It is as if God has been pushed aside, out of the center of Abraham's world, and is no longer a prime mover in his life. Earthly love leaves no room for any significant relationship with the divinity. After Satan sows the seeds of doubt, God attempts to reclaim his exclusive position in Abraham's psychic life. He can do so by removing Isaac, the human factor that has entered the relationship between Abraham and God and usurped God's status there. But Isaac can only be removed through the imposition of an inhuman demand that will reestablish what God considers the correct priorities: God first and foremost, and human relations thereafter. God needs a man who will be prepared to give up his humanity as proof of God's order of priorities. God is jealous of the love Abraham has for his son, is anxious about his place in Abraham's soul, and tries to resolve the situation by dismissing the object of human love. God must prove to himself his exclusivity in Abraham's life.

This attribute of a "jealous God" can be nullified by introducing the human element into God by way of sacrificing it to God. Isaac has human attributes. By sacrificing these, it is as if God is able to relate to the humane, to the imperfect—to human beings. The moment Abraham is ready to sacrifice Isaac and his love for him, and through him his continuation into posterity, God gains a new exclusivity in Abraham's life. This is indeed proof of the sublime importance of God, an importance exceeding Abraham's own life and that of his son, and of his ability to relegate the institution of human love to its proper place, between people over whom God reigns. Thus God is satisfied, and the proper scale of priorities is restored. For love belongs only to the domain of relations between mortals in this story.

Thus far the biblical account reflects the struggle for precedence within Abraham's psyche between ego and Self, which dominates Abraham with its inhuman demands. Once the ego is sacrificed on the altar of the Self, human psychic attributes permeate the Self, which acquires traits represented by the ego. Thereby the ego as well as the Self expands, and, thus, the individual's personality. These events are the supreme manifestation of the dynamic of change that occurs in the internal struggles, relinquishings, and sacrifices of the human mind.

The human psyche is the battleground of the forces that act within and upon it. As Jung comments, "The archetype of the self has, functionally, the significance of a ruler of the inner world, i.e., of the collective unconscious. The self, as a symbol of wholeness, is a *coincidentia oppositorum*, and therefore contains light and darkness simultaneously" (1956, par. 576). The relationship between the ego and the Self may be compared to that between moved and mover; the two parts of the mind are always interdependent and interrelated. Elsewhere, Jung elaborates:

> The energy of the archetype communicates itself to the ego only when the latter has been influenced or gripped by an autonomous action of the archetype. From this psychological fact one would have to conclude that the man who practices a spiritual form of love has already been gripped by something akin to a *donum gratiae*, for he could hardly be expected to be capable of usurping, on his own resources, a divine action such as that love is. But by virtue of the *donum amoris* he becomes capable of taking God's place in this respect. It is a psychological fact that an archetype can seize hold of the ego and even compel it to act as it—the archetype—wills. A man can then take on archetypal dimensions and exercise corresponding effects; he can appear in the place of God. (1956, par. 101)

Everything stated generally with regard to the archetype applies even more to the archetype of the Self.

Further interpretation may be necessary to understand the

phrase "God tried Abraham." "Tried" means that the Self has confronted Abraham with what may be the harshest experience of all: the renunciation of human egocentrism, the forsaking of the ego that views itself as the mover of and the agent responsible for all processes.

Satan's statements, as presented in the *aggadah*, allude to Abraham's failure to express gratitude to God for the miracle visited upon him. Humility may have surrendered to self-aggrandizement, admiration of his own ability to cause the miracle. Egocentric arrogance engulfs him. Admittedly, Abraham has had good reason thus far to experience God as a benefactor only, because his contacts with God have been limited to role exchanges and interdependency. He is only human, undergoing processes that fuel his arrogance, making him credit his experiences and achievements to himself and his own powers. With Satan's words, the hand of the shadow—the wreaking of evil in the service of good—becomes visible. Delusions of grandeur are common, as is the deflating of the personality to achieve basic human modesty, the recognition of human finiteness and limitations.

The inflation of Abraham's personality makes it necessary for the voice of the Self to be heard, demanding the killing of the son as a symbol of his being mortal, not divine. This outburst of aggression against the son, who evidently competes for his position, is another manifestation of Abraham's fears of a diminishing of his power, requiring the intervention of the inner voice.

Feelings of aggression are manifestations of regressive situations. Abraham withdraws to a world in which human sacrifice is prevalent and predominant—to his world before the consciousness that dawned after the first "get thee forth" in Genesis 12, which led to the second "get thee forth" in Genesis 22.2. The latter ostensibly clashes with the consciousness that has developed within him, but is accessible to him only in the deepest, most primitive area of his psyche. He must experience this consciousness, awaken to its existence, and arise from it cleansed, pure, and aware of the God within him. Regression to the world of childhood—to the pagan world where the child Abraham feels safe, where his father and family determine events, where there are no vacillations, no doubts, no responsibilities, and no struggles, to the protection and the comfort that prevail there—is a well-known pattern of psychological behavior. At the same time, withdrawal (as to the cave, identified above as a symbol of the unknown; as to the mother's womb, safe from all harm) serves the process of individuation, just as the shadow often may assist this vital process. From the place of refuge (the womb, the cave) emanates power, the source of the psychic vitality and strength needed to cope with the labors a person must perform in the course of individuation. One who musters this strength is one who summons the courage to break out of the vicious circle of the Great Mother. The mythical world, a reflection of the deepest levels of the psyche—the world of archetypes—presents numerous accounts of heroes who withdraw to one of the unconscious symbols of the Great Mother, where they are reborn and then emerge with the powers needed to tackle the tasks facing them. Thus regression is used to store and marshal spiritual energy for a struggle with fate.

The mythical sphere is therefore attached to the unconscious. With respect to the mythical hero (and to our understanding of Abraham as a mythical hero), Jung writes:

> The hero myth is an unconscious drama seen only in projection, like the happenings in Plato's parable of the cave. The hero himself appears as a being of more than human stature. He is distinguished from the very beginning by his godlike characteristics. Since he is psychologically an archetype of the self, his divinity only confirms that the self is numinous. . . . For psychology the self is an imago Dei and cannot be distinguished from it empirically. (1956, par. 612)

It is in view of this truth that we have written this study.

We return to the biblical account. "[Take] that which you love and get thee out to the land of Moriah." The command "get thee out," uttered at the beginning of the story, is repeated. "Get thee out" means embarking on a new life with a new concept of the divinity. "Get thee out" means expressing a willingness to accept constant change. It means sacrificing old truths and moving toward a new inner truth, toward an awareness of the existence of deeper, more arduous and demanding psychic levels—those of the personality developing in the awareness of their existence. It is no coincidence that the phrase occurs at the beginning, when the divine command is first heard, and toward the end. In both instances, Abraham is required to make a dramatic change in his way of life, his thinking, and the setting of standards for his personality. The binding of

Isaac marks the climax of Abraham's new life, begun with the first "get thee out" and nearly extinct with its repetition.

Abraham undergoes a complete transformation in these two episodes. The first necessarily leads to the second, as dictated by the dynamic of personal change. One who starts with change must continue to change by virtue of his willingness to change. Being open to change in this way is essential to the process of individuation.

"Get thee into the land of Moriah; and offer him there as for a burnt-offering upon one of the mountains." In the ancient world, mountains were deemed the representatives of the gods. Mountains embody the strength and power of nature, as if they are conduits by which heaven and earth meet. Through them the corporeal and the spiritual connect. Perhaps because of the numinous feeling and the sensation of approaching the power that it emanates, the mountain is chosen as the place for the rite of serving God. It is as if by ascending, by exerting himself to reach its summit, a person manifests the willingness to draw closer to God. It is no coincidence that the most significant divine revelation in the history of the people of Israel occurred at Mount Sinai, and that, despite very marked differences, the pantheon of Greek pagan deities was on Mount Olympus. In the biblical account of the binding of Isaac, no particular mountain is specified. ("Upon one of the mountains in the land of Moriah"). By this, the deity may have wished to avoid sanctifying a specific mountain and making it the object of a "mountain rite." Perhaps, too, the divinity is universal and transient, like Abraham himself, impulsive when it comes to determining and deciding where the sacrifice will be held.

It was only after Judaism was institutionalized that the mountain and the land of Moriah were identified as the abode of God and the site of the Temple, where institutionalized rites were performed. We concur with the understanding that "the land of Moriah" is Jerusalem, for Jerusalem is nestled in mountains where the spiritual center of divine worship once stood.

"And offer him there for a burnt-offering" (Hebrew, *'olah*). The type of offering—a burnt offering, one that is utterly consumed—is specified, and the root of the term, *A-L-H*, whence *'aliya* (ascent) is derived. Not only does the burnt offering ascend to the heavens, so does the person making the sacrifice, identifying with it as it approaches the divinity.

"On the third day Abraham lifted up his eyes and saw the place from afar" (Gen. 22.4). We have already discussed the significance of the number three, the reason that Abraham was given three days, not four or two. The mountain chosen by God for the Binding was revealed on the third day. Rashi asks: "Why did He not show Abraham the mountain at once?" He answers: "So it would not be said that he was suddenly terrified, disturbed, and deranged, but that had he been allowed time to reconsider, he would not have acted."

Rashi construed the respite given Abraham from the time he received the divine command until its execution as a period of time meant for Abraham to weigh his actions and perform them in full consciousness, not on the basis of a spontaneous, uncontrolled impulse—a regressive, aggressive impulse, which he calls "becoming deranged." In Jungian psychology, derangement occurs when the unconscious dominates the ego.

The possibility of reconsidering arises during this time. Abraham has the opportunity to cope with his desire to escape from this terrible task and to regret having agreed to offer his son as a sacrifice to God. The respite also allows Abraham to examine himself, to digest and understand the meaning of the sacrifice, and to prepare to carry it out. These days, presumably among the worst of Abraham's life, are replete with struggle and vacillation between his love for his son and his desire to keep him alive, and his submission to the divine command and the negation of his physical love, which entails the negation—more precisely, the elimination—of himself. The biblical account says nothing about what is in Abraham's mind. The episode of the Binding would be reduced in stature if it were played out immediately in a spirit of derangement, of religious ecstasy following the encounter with the divine—the command heard by Abraham directly.

Various civilizations inform us of the human ability, when a person is in a hypnotic state ("disturbed and deranged") to perform acts not possible when that person is fully conscious. (Consider the actions of *fakirs* or of Shiites in religious processions.) However, the account of the Binding insists on the prevention of this psychic state. The sacrifice must be performed in full consciousness, with an awareness of the extent of the sacrifice and the personal devotion demanded to carry it out.

Previously, Abraham would have replied to God, arguing and even bargaining with him. This time, he says nothing, requests nothing, demands no explanation. He does not bargain with God. He listens and sets out to act. Perhaps God suspects Abraham's readiness to obey, sensing that Abraham is in a state of mystic perception, a religious ecstasy devoid of the ability to reflect and the consciousness needed to understand and approve of the divine demand. Hence respite is provided. A sacrifice based on an unconscious drive is not a sacrifice but rather the fulfillment of an instinctive aggression—a regression to the earliest stages of human consciousness.

This is not what God wants; he desires a conscious sacrifice. Only a conscious renunciation of that which is most precious will be accepted, only willingness following vacillation, negating any possibility of spontaneous action, represents the conscious submission to and acceptance of the yoke of divine command that emanates from the Self and is processed consciously by the ego, even if it jeopardizes the one who is, in fact, sacrificing himself. Abraham's migration and search for the mountain where the Binding is to take place are thus a search for consciousness, a negation of doubt, a relinquishing of love, a denial of and a departure from simple humanity. This is the reason for the three days Abraham was given.

Once the mountain is in sight, Abraham takes leave of his "young men" at the bottom of the slopes and advances, carrying the knife and the fire, with Isaac, who bears wood on his back. The two ascend the mountain alone, for this sacrifice must be performed in total privacy. The communion with God and its attendant agony cannot be borne in the company of spectators. Each soul in this situation, with its sublime tension, and apprehension, must be an active participant. The "young men" are therefore superfluous.

There may be another reason for their absence. "We shall come back to you," Abraham promises the young men. He fears that if they know the real reason for the journey, they will try to prevent his carrying out the deed. Or he may fear that if they plead for Isaac's life his own determination may waver. Perhaps he is afraid that human love and compassion will overwhelm his submission to God.

There is yet another consideration for the exclusion of the young men: they are not of a status that permits their participation in this rite of supreme and most holy sacrifice, which must be performed far from onlookers, in the Holy of Holies, not in a sanctuary accessible to the masses. According to the *aggadah*, this mountain subsequently became the site of the Temple and the Holy of Holies; the *d'vir* (sanctuary), the room entered only by the High Priest, was erected where Abraham's altar stood. It is more likely, however, that Abraham does not wish the young men to dissuade him from carrying out the action for which he has had to marshal vast psychic resources. He can do this only in a state of privacy. To carry out this internal imperative, he must be alone during his hour of trial.

"And they went both of them together" (Gen. 22.6). It is not grammatically necessary to use the term *together*; the meaning and substance of the sentence would be the same if it simply read "and the two of them went." *Together* seems to have been added to emphasize the unequivocal assertion that the account is presenting us with a single being in two separate bodies. Ascending to the site of the binding together, Abraham and Isaac become a unit comprising the conscious figure of the father and the unconscious figure of the son.

Like God, father and son are active parts of Abraham's psyche, for he embodies the father, the son, and the divine command at one and the same time. He contains divine dynamism, the love of the father, and the submission of the son, and each of these psychic components is in conflict within him. A most terrible human drama is taking place because the One who demands the sacrifice, the one who is to perform the sacrifice, and the sacrifice itself are identical. Thus the account uses the word *together* although each one is, in fact, the victim of the other.

Abraham is the victim of God, subject to and controlled by the demands of the deity, although as a man he presumably protests God's inhuman demands. Isaac is Abraham's sacrifice in his unconscious. Both are victims of the power and the pernicious dynamism emanating from Abraham's Self. Were the sacrifice actually to occur, it would destroy itself and its agents. Abraham represents the submissive son before the divinity in its aggressive embodiment—the Great Father—just as Isaac is the helpless son unable to cope with his own father's rage. In other words, the sacrificer and the victim are the two facets of the archetype of sacrifice. The sacrifice is demanded by the Self—the forces of the psyche, the archetypal center of the personality, which are one and the same.

We find this psychic mechanism difficult to understand because it is hard for us to separate the aggressor—the one making the sacrifice—from the victim, to accept that both are present within us and act through the prompting of the supreme command, which is also within. This mechanism may be more easily understood if it is rephrased thus: Abraham prepares to sacrifice Isaac as an expression of his aggressive aspect, just as he himself is a victim of divine aggression, which is also an aspect of his personality. In this, he is like Isaac. The voice of God, issuing its commands, is the Self—the eternal element of Abraham's psyche, the aggressor. The Self, however, is also the victim of the voice ordering Abraham to be as submissive to him as Isaac the son, the object of Abraham's sublime yearning, is treasured as the vehicle of Abraham's eternity as part of the Self.

Thus, in terms of the value of eternity in Abraham's psyche, God and Isaac are identical as active components. Abraham's soul is acted upon by a dynamic of divine eternity composed of victim and aggressor. All are alive, and their existence and vitality depend on him.

Abraham's psyche is a stage for these battling forces. The terrible conflict is that all of them are parts of himself. Abraham, who obeys the call of the Self, expresses his aggression. His submission represents Isaac's submission to God and himself. Thus Abraham and Isaac are the victims of God as much as they are symbolic parts of the God-image, which appears as the voice of the Self. Abraham, the sacrifice/sacrificer, is aware of the power of the Self, and accepts its domination and the fact of its supremacy. He is aware of the enormity of the sacrifice he must make, and it is to become aware that the interlude is given him. He experiences the most dreadful vacillations. Then, consciously, he decides to carry out the sacrifice of Isaac—to relinquish his perpetuity, his Self, the dynamic facet of God within him. Once he decides to comply, his surrender is total.

The nullification of his humane essence before God is a terrifying human experience. It is also numinous; Rudolf Otto, in *The Idea of the Holy* (1959), defines it as "awe"—literally, the "fear of God." Thus Abraham changes, and, with him, so does the God-image. The numinous experience is an acceptance of the opposites. The view of the Self as whole and as containing opposites—this is the paradox of God and the experiencing of God. Fear, anxiety, and compassion—human attributes that must be overcome in order to make as great a sacrifice as Abraham's—infuse the divinity with the human element symbolized by these attributes.

"And Abraham took the wood of the burnt-offering and laid it on Isaac his son" (Gen. 22.6). It is altogether natural that the young man should carry the wood. However, it is difficult to avoid making

94

the association with the symbolic act described by the *aggadah* as "bearing the crucified one on his shoulder" (Bialik and Ravnitzki 1951, Ma'asei Avot 45). The inference is to the placing of suffering, which leads to oblivion, on the shoulders of the lamb set aside for the burnt offering.

Isaac carries the wood, Abraham the fire and the knife. The wood of the burnt offering symbolizes the life that will ascend and be consumed; the fire and the knife the destructive force that will consume it. Observing these preparations, "Isaac said to Abraham his father, saying, 'My father,' and he said, 'Here am I, my son,' and he said, 'Behold the fire and the wood; but where is the lamb for a burnt-offering?'" (Gen. 22.7). Abraham replies: "'God will provide Himself the lamb for a burnt-offering, my son,' and they went on together" (22.8). Isaac asks a simple question; Abraham replies evasively.

Here the question of Isaac's age arises. At what age does a person accept a vague, evasive reply without inquiring further? The *Midrash Genesis Rabbah* (1951) debates the question, some Sages arguing that Isaac was thirteen years old, others that he was thirty-seven. No unequivocal ruling is given. Many artists have depicted Isaac as a boy. If so, however, how could he carry a load of wood sufficient to consume a human body, even a small one? We therefore may deduce that Isaac is an adult.

The perception of Isaac as a child, however, is understandable. Not only does the connection between the accounts of his birth and of the binding identify him as young in years; so, too, does the extent of his passivity in blindly following his father. Whether Isaac is an adult or a child, his psychological age is such that his father is still the supreme authority figure, in whom he has perfect, unshakable faith.

If his physical age and strength allow him to carry a load of wood, he therefore must be able to draw conclusions and raise objections, but, according to the biblical account, Isaac accepts his father's words meekly, without reflection. He is described as a childish and passive personality who obeys his father submissively, unthinkingly—a portrait that did not change much throughout his life, according to the biblical account. In the *aggadah* and *midrashim*, however, the Sages sought virtue in his passivity, interpreting it as a profound religious-mystical experience that penetrates the upper worlds. Thus, for example, "When Isaac lay down on the altar, the gates of the heavens opened, and Isaac saw the angels from above weeping for the fate of the father and his son" (*Midrash Genesis Rabbah*; Bialik and Ravnitzki 1951). There, tears fell on Isaac's eyes and were the reason for his becoming blind in his old age ("And his eyes were dim," Gen. 27.1).

"And Abraham built the altar there, and laid the wood in order, and bound Isaac his son, and laid him upon the altar, upon the wood. And he stretched forth his hand, and took the knife to slay his son" (Gen. 22.9–10). The narrative is straightforward, dry, precise. There is a parallel reference to "Isaac his son," as well as another reference to "his son," to avoid the impression that Abraham has taken some other Isaac.

It is a detailed account, presented in simple words, describing actions in sequence, ascending to the climax. Tension is generated by the contrast between the words and the actions they describe— the laconic, measured words stand in contrast to this horrifying episode, so charged with emotion. The effect is an awesome human drama endowed with defined human concepts that are unbearable to the psyche, defying our comprehension and grasp.

"And Abraham stretched forth his hand, and took the knife to slay his son" (Gen. 22.10). Can one imagine a more terrible atrocity than this, albeit for the loftiest purpose? What must have transpired in the heart of the father about to slay his son, thereby destroying his future and with it himself?

It is clear beyond all doubt, however, that such an emotional state also serves to obstruct the simple human feelings that must stir within Abraham when he is in a normal mental state. For Abraham is on the border between sanity and insanity. He has lost his self-control. He is prey to destructive impulses. That he is on the edge, however, implies another possibility—that his personality may regain its equilibrium, its emotional perspective, its psychic balance. If so, the vast psychic powers within the person can be channeled into something constructive and positive. Indeed, this is what happens at the end of the biblical account of the Binding.

The blocking of emotions can be autosuggestive—a kind of emotional anesthesia meant to stifle pain or other emotion. Perhaps Abraham is running amok, impelled by an undiagnosed instinct of destruction that advances indiscriminately and ultimately harms the body, as almost happens here. Abraham is in a state of fanatical religious ecstasy, his link with reality severed. In this state, he makes contact with the Self, negating himself in the face of a spiritual experience that completely overtakes him. The laws that previously acted upon him are no longer valid.

In light of the amount of aggression expressed in the attempted slaughter, all three possibilities mentioned above are part of Abraham's psyche at this particular moment. Could it be that the passage of the three days given him allowed him to anesthetize himself and to prepare himself for an emotional exit from human bondage? The moment that Abraham grasps the knife—the symbol of the reaper, of death—to carry out the act of slaughter, the moment the aggressive emotion reaches its climax, it is nullified. The touch of the knife mitigates his fervor and permits the voice of the angel of the Lord, the voice of the Self, to be heard.

Symbolically, the knife separates the destructive impulse from the person it controls. Sanity is regained, and a new life becomes possible. Thus the symbol of death embodies the symbol of the renewal of hope and redemption; it also represents the change that is the goal of the Binding.

"And the Angel of the Lord called unto him" (Gen. 22.11). The voice of the angel penetrates the emotional maelstrom within Abraham. The voice overcomes the impenetrability, the deafness, the blindness that signify ecstatic emotion. The voice emanates from the Self; it is the innermost voice, identified with the voice of God, the voice of sanity, the voice that demands cessation—"Lay not thy hand upon the lad" (Gen. 22.12)—that demands the sacrifice be halted. The inner voice that previously demanded the sacrifice of Isaac is the same voice that now demands the nullification of the sacrifice.

Ten

Implications of the Binding

Let us bear in mind that every change begins with aggression against the old order, which either makes way for the new order or serves as its foundation. Aggression originates in discontent and thus may be construed as a form of energy that can be used positively once it is released. Once the aggression is exhausted, the old is destroyed and the energy flows in positive channels. In the episode of the Binding, when Abraham grasps the knife, the aggression reaches its peak. The rite is virtually complete, to the most minute detail. On the brink of the most terrible of human crimes—self-destruction—the change takes place within Abraham, and, therefore, within the divine image as well. The face of compassion—the angel of the Lord, who overcomes the divinity as a result of Abraham's utter submission—is the one that insists on terminating the slaughter.

Identifying the angel of the Lord as the divinity is dictated by the text: "And the angel of the Lord called" (Gen. 22.15). "By Myself have I sworn, saith the Lord" (Gen. 22.16) is phrased in the first person singular, indicating that the speakers are one. "And he said, 'Here am I.' " Again, the stress is on Abraham's readiness to obey the Lord's changing and opposing demands—submissively and with a maximum of self-exposure: here am I before you, at your disposal, exposed and known, ready and amenable. "Lay not thy hand on the lad . . . for now I know that thou art a God-fearing man, seeing thou hast not withheld thy son, thine only son, from Me" (Gen. 22.12). Here, the willingness expressed in Abraham's reply also manifests the ebbing of the initial aggression, the obfuscation of the senses that thus far has overwhelmed him. The consciousness expressed in the words "Here am I" symbolizes the transition and the separation from oblivion of the senses, and the mystical identity between man and the world, to reality and a new consciousness—a consciousness that provides the ram.

On their way to the mountain, Isaac asks his father, "But where is the lamb for a burnt-offering?" The lamb—a symbol of innocence, meekness, conformity—was not provided. Isaac was the only lamb in this scene, and as such prefigures Jesus. Instead, God provides a ram—a symbol of coarse, brutish, instinctive male sexuality, of unrestrained aggression and impulsiveness—for a sacrifice admirably suited to all the repressed feelings that are about to surface and overwhelm the participants.

The *aggadah* relates that the ram sacrificed in Isaac's stead was created during the six days of Creation. One indication of its primeval nature, as manifested in its impulsiveness, is found in a Persian legend that blames the ram for tempting Adam and Eve. Like the snake, a phallic symbol, the ram is a symbol of sexuality. It is thus perceived in the Egyptian pantheon—the husband of the goddess Tamahit. The best-known manifestation of the ram symbol is the Hittite ram god (with which some associate the Hebrew word for the divinity, *El = eyal = ayil* = "ram"— power and strength). As a result of what was said, each of those taking part in the scene of the binding, God and man, had to give up and sacrifice the aggression that the ram symbolizes.

Abraham's total willingness to sacrifice his son ("Seeing thou hast not withheld thy son") eliminates the need to do so. God won the human element that Abraham sacrificed for his sake. God's aspect of human compassion and loving-kindness is revealed and expressed by his stopping the sacrifice. God, as it were, is aware of the aggression within him and thus relinquishes it. It is then that the voice of the angel of the Lord is heard, giving the command for life. Instead of Isaac, the lamb, the aggressive facets of the human being and God are symbolically sacrificed in the offering of the ram, and the divine image is cleansed. God provides the ram as a symbol of himself, sacrificing it to himself through Abraham and forgoing the sacrifice of the lamb—Isaac.

It is quite possible that the Binding was a drama enacted to abolish human sacrifice. It follows that in Abraham's state of regression and unconsciousness during the binding, he returns to his childhood and the attitudes of the pagan world, in which human sacrifice was prevalent. Thus sacrificing the ram is a symbol of the sacrificing of the pagan world, to which, for one moment in his process of psychic retreat, Abraham almost surrenders.

The account of the Binding opens with "And they went both of them together" (Gen. 22.6) and closes with "So Abraham returned unto his young men" (22.19). Note the use of the singular in the final verse of the account; is it an oversight or perhaps a spelling mistake? Maybe, as *Midrash Genesis Rabbah* relates, Isaac is in fact sacrificed as a burnt offering and dies on the altar (1951). According to the *aggadah*, he is the lamb of the burnt offering, and only when his ashes are sprinkled with dew is he restored to life (Bialik and Ravnitzki 1951). Clearly, it was the erroneous use of the singular that gave the Sages the opportunity to present this *aggadah*. Perhaps, too, the biblical account is the emended version: Abraham does return alone to his young men, and Isaac is indeed sacrificed, slaughtered on the altar, and then brought back to life when anointed by the dew, as the *aggadah* relates. This is a common theme in legends: the story of a son or daughter offered as a sacrifice to appease the gods' wrath of the gods against humanity—a deed that may be defined as the archetype of sacrifice in its primeval form.

Another version of "Abraham returned unto his young men," without Isaac, could be because Isaac has become one of the components of Abraham's psyche. He ignored Isaac, who is no longer a separate being—childish, submissive, unconscious—but present and alive. Abraham has internalized Isaac so thoroughly that he cannot perceive Isaac's existence as real. In the state of mind Abraham was in at that moment, Isaac became part of the totality of his psyche, with its many facts and contradictions. He has been nullified as an independent being. In other words, Abraham's experience of the act of sacrifice is so complete that, for him, Isaac, the son, has ceased to exist, becoming instead part of that component of Abraham's psyche that was sacrificed to God. Thus Abraham returns alone.

There is another possible interpretation, which is the opposite of the previous: Abraham has sacrificed the projections he has cast upon Isaac, and is now freed from Isaac as part of his psyche. From now on, Isaac is an independent being who exists in his own right. Abraham's integrity and wholeness are enhanced by his forfeiting Isaac and his grip on him. Abraham must acknowledge the need to renounce his parental projections onto his son, thus allowing Isaac to live not as his parents' child but as an independent being.

One of the climaxes of the process of individuation—for Abraham as for anyone—is the sacrifice of projections, the relinquishing of control over and expectations of another person, the ability to dissociate oneself from the object of one's projections. Abraham embarks on this terrible episode bearing the burden of Isaac's life (projection), and returns to his young men as one—different, whole, aware that he has parted with Isaac forever. Thus he returns alone.

"For now I know that thou art a God-fearing man" (Gen. 22.12). The concept of "God-fearing" requires explanation. In its straightforward, conventional sense, it means someone who is afraid of God (as in Proverbs 28.14—"Happy is the man that feareth always"; from the root *P-H-D*). The fear in Genesis 22.12, however, is *yira*, a combination of fear and honor. It is by virtue of honor that Abraham may relate to God with the respect that originates in the conscious mind. Fear, by contrast, belongs to the level of reaction to that which provokes the fear. To construe *yira* as ordinary fear is to belittle the magnitude of Abraham's sacrifice to God.

A frightened person usually reacts instinctively. For Abraham, however, the interval provided him (or taken by him), in which he works through the experience of the command, indicates that a concept of divinity driven by fear is not desirable, that an approach based on respect, conscious understanding, and sacrifice—the terms embraced by *yira*—is more honorable, indeed, superior.

Unlike the term *God-fearing* (awe), "Isaac's fright," which some think is the private name of Isaac's divinity (how appropriate a name for a God as fearful as the one he experienced), leaves no grounds for understanding in the context of cognition. Isaac's fear is existential. His life is in danger. Abraham's physical self is not in danger, but his existence as the bearer of the divine projection of a father to a nation—his future existence—is surely in jeopardy. No doubt, Abraham felt himself dying with the threat of his son's death. He identifies emotionally, as any father would, but his physical being is assured. The God-fearing Abraham is in awe of and honors the God who speaks to him. In so doing, he honors the voice emanating from the Self, the divine image as an integral part of his psyche.

The path along which Abraham's life develops, which leads to this integration of all the elements of his personality and his efforts to deal with the unconscious aspects thereof, reaches its climax with the dramatic act of the Binding. After this, it is impossible to attain greater heights of understanding or delve deeper into the psyche.

Eleven

The Symbol of the Shofar—The Ram's Horn

Abraham lives and begets other sons. However, the rest of the biblical account (Gen. 25) shows that these offspring are unimportant to him; he dismisses them with gifts and nothing more. It should perhaps be noted that Isaac and Ishmael meet again when Abraham is buried (Gen. 25.9). This last reunion may be significant with regard to two brothers of such opposing mythical significance. After this, however, they part forever.

Let us now return to the episode of the Binding. Isaac is prostrate, bound on the altar, either crying for help but heard by no one, his father offering no compassion, or lying helpless, paralyzed with fear. Abraham grips the knife with trembling hands (or the certainty of the frenzy of the fanatical believer). His eyes glare frightfully (or brim with tears for the life he is about to obliterate). The atmosphere is replete with instincts of destruction and perdition. The world holds its breath; there is neither the slightest stir nor rustle, no hint of compassion. The only sound is the crackling of the fire consuming the wood. Heat and terror prevail in a vision of horror and atrocity. It may be a sacrifice to God, but murder is about to be committed. Then the voice is heard, commanding that the sacrifice be stopped, the aspect of compassion is revealed in God, and the ram comes into view, to be slaughtered in Isaac's stead. The tension dissipates. Abraham, his God, and his honor have been saved. The animal in the thicket carries the burden and is sacrificed.

In psychological terms, Abraham is in a stage of human development corresponding to puberty—a stage at which adolescents test the limits of life. It is a psychic state charged with an unbearable amount of aggression, which must find its outlet in some aggressive act. Youngsters test their strength with various kinds of heroic actions, ranging from rebellion against the authority of parents, teachers, and political regimes to attempted suicide and even playing the deadly game of Russian roulette. Abraham, who is in an aggressive state, is directed by an uncontrolled urge to destroy his son. He must kill, so overwhelmed is he by the tumult of emotions that has been created by his extreme aggressive impulses.

Then, unexpectedly, Abraham notices the ram caught in the thicket. It is as if the divinity in its aggressive aspect is actually present before him. The symbol of the aggressive God who has commanded the human sacrifices of Abraham and Isaac materializes, caught in a thicket, helpless, unable to do any harm—God offering himself as an alternate victim to Isaac. The ram's advent is a divine or magic coincidence, a synchronistic situation, an unexpected meaningful occurrence for Abraham during his state of great emotion: the concurrence of a given psychic state and an event or events that meaningfully correspond to a momentary objective situation.

Such coincidence is either a connecting noncausal principle or meaningfully linked but causally unrelated events. In a state of extreme emotional turmoil, his senses suspended, Abraham discovers the ram. Utterly blind to life's realities, he is prey to the impulse to annihilate, to destroy his life and the life of his son. Nevertheless, he is still able to distinguish a reality beyond himself: the objective reality of the ram caught in the thicket. He is able to recognize the presence of a real animal, which he may sacrifice instead of his son. Thus he is able to muster the psychic forces required to switch from one frame of mind to another, to sacrifice the ram instead of Isaac. In psychological terms, Abraham is able to distinguish between the inner impulse and the sacrifice itself: he is capable of moving from the unconscious domain in which he is prey to destructive instincts to the consciousness that is necessary for him to be able to choose the sacrifice.

This new ability changes Abraham, and thus the image of his God. Abraham objectivizes the aggression within him and summons reserves of psychic strength in order to direct this aggression at the ram, the symbol of the aggressive side of God. The picture of the ram caught fast in the thicket represents the change in substance that has occurred in Abraham's perception of the divinity, in his conceptualization of the divine.

With the appearance of the ram, not only does God become nonaggressive but there is also an essential change, a shift to a different stage of development, in which God becomes his own victim. (Any aggression ultimately harms the aggressor.) This is the archetypal picture of God sacrificing himself, one that has acquired an extreme form in the Christian attitude toward the divinity, which views God in his human embodiment as a victim. This motif also appears in other myths, such as those of Attis and Mithras, and in an Icelandic saga telling the story of Odin, who sacrifices himself to himself ("Suspended from the branches of a tree, for nine days and nine nights I sacrificed myself to myself.")

Abraham, having sacrificed the aggressive facet of God within him and killed the magic beast, the ram (which the Sages say was created at the creation of the world), now acquires something of its tremendous strength, as Jung notes. As a result, Abraham is able to dissociate himself from the mystic feeling of unity with the world, of being one with the universe, utterly absorbed into nature (*participation mystique*). Thus he succeeds in attaining the separation that distinguishes human beings from nature, by breaking the stranglehold of the unconscious on his actions within the terrible and splendid numinous episode that overcomes him.

The sacrifice of the ram is the anticlimax of the violent drama of the binding. From now on, events move into Abraham's consciousness, and he is no longer dominated by the archetype of sacrifice. The binding marks the start of Abraham's ability to see the ram's existence as a reality external to himself. The various parts of the mind—God, Abraham, Isaac, and the ram—now claim their existence as independent beings. Thus Abraham is able to pay due respect to them and their existence within his Self, as well as being able to provide them with an outlet and a resolution consistent with his cultural-ethical system.

We have already noted that emotional regression is often necessary in the process of individuation. The Binding, the climax of Abraham's emotional-conceptual development, is, we believe, a regressive episode needed in order for Abraham to be able to examine the various parts of his psyche. Abraham can thereby purify himself of vestiges of the past to help him acknowledge his shadow, free himself from projections, and open the way for further development and correct use of the energy released in this process. Let us not forget that human sacrifice, especially of children, was a custom in the culture from which Abraham came and of the culture in the area at the time.

The emotional charge accumulated during the Binding is released with the sacrifice of the ram. The ram, the symbol of the aggressive and destructive side of God, is sacrificed to God. The ram's horn contains the essence of the ram's symbolic attributes; the *shofar*, a highly significant symbol in Jewish tradition and prayer, is made from a ram's horn. The *shofar* is discussed below in conjunction with the multiple aspects and uses of horns, as a result of their direct connection with the episode of the Binding. For, even as it symbolizes human-divine aggression, the horn is also a symbol of atonement, regeneration, and hope.

J. Scheftelowitz (1912, p. 451ff.), asserts that the early godheads, which had animal forms, expressed the inhuman power in God (1912, p. 451ff). Such gods often were represented by the image of a ram. The horns that adorned the heads of idols are vestiges of images of the early godhead, expressing power, might, and at the same time active defense against the forces of evil.

The ram's horn thus has emerged into human consciousness as a sign worthy of respect. It is a natural symbol of power and strength, coupled with aggressiveness, that arouses fear and awe— all of which typify the animal itself. Because the horn is located on the head of the animal-god, people respect it. (Consider the birth of Pallas Athene from the head of Zeus.) The Vikings also used the horn as a symbol of power and honor, possibly as well to frighten their enemies. They fastened the horns to their helmets.

The Bible refers to the horn as a manifestation of dignity, if in a humbled form ("I have sewed sackcloth upon my skin, and have laid my horn in the dust"—Job 16.15). As a symbol of the divine strength embodied in the horn—strength that can serve as a gateway of hope and salvation—the animal horn becomes the "corner of the altar," a place where the inadvertent sinner can plead for life. The horn was used to store the oil with which kings were anointed (I Samuel 16.13). The Bible contains many references to the horn, including figurative expressions alluding to strength, vigor, and valor.

Only once does the Bible use the word *qeren* (horn) as a synonym for *shofar* (ram's horn): "And it shall be, that when they make a long blast with the ram's horn" (Joshua 6.5). The ram's horn is a natural symbol for the Binding, and it is in this context that we shall discuss it and its archetypal meaning and use in Jewish tradition.

The horn on the ram's head points upward, reminiscent of a male (phallic) symbol of aggression. As a receptacle, it is also a female symbol. The *shofar* is thus a multifaceted symbol, coupling male and female, material and spiritual. It is a symbol of wholeness, of the reconciliation of opposites.

The *shofar's* material aspect is its physical substance. The *shofar's* spiritual aspect is represented by the blowing of air—the spirit being drawn in—a human act which imbues matter with the intangible, which makes audible things that exist and do not exist, things heard but not seen, like the divinity itself. The sounding of the *shofar* is an embodiment, so to speak, of the immense power and force of God, of God's presence in the here and now. Even today, the sounding of the *shofar* sends shivers down one's spine. The *shofar* is a symbol of transcendental, archetypal energy; it causes a numinous sensation. The effect of the *shofar* on the listener has been known since time immemorial and it thus has been used for various purposes, on which we shall elaborate.

The *shofar* may be the oldest musical instrument. Made of the ram's horn and perceived as a manifestation of the divinity's menacing strength and ability to intimidate, the *shofar* has been endowed with forces of its own—forces that can perform magic and change the laws of nature. In psychological terms, the performance of a magic rite, or the use of elements that evoke a magical sensation, endows the believer with an increased feeling of security. Such rites maintain a person's psychic equilibrium in the early developmental stages, before one is aware of the laws of nature. All ritual contains an element of magic; to this day vestiges of it survive in the use of the *shofar* and the significance projected upon it.

In "The Shofar," Sol B. Finesinger asserts that "vocalization and the emission of noises are magic devices meant to permit human beings to impose light on darkness (the forces of good on the forces of evil and obscurity, the absence of consciousness). The role of men is to come to divinity's assistance." (1931–32, p. 194). Erich Neumann comments that "the magical effect of the rite is factual enough . . . it actually works out, . . . The magical rite, like all magic and indeed every higher intention, including those of religion, acts upon the subject who practices the magic or the religion, by altering and enhancing his own ability to act. . . . In this sense the outcome of the action . . . is in the highest degree objectively dependent upon the effect of the magical ritual. . . . The operative factor in magic is the reality of the soul. . . ." (1954, p. 209). In other words, the emission of voices and sounds—in our case, the sounding of the *shofar*—forces the believer to change, thereby augmenting that person's ability to shape and deal with reality.

The most striking example of magic that modifies laws and realities, and which is embodied in the sounding of the *shofar* and its use as a component of ritual, is the conquest of Jericho. There is also evidence that until the end of the nineteenth century, the *shofar* was blown in order to drive out demons and spirits that were believed to dwell within people, as in the exorcism of the *dybbuk.*

The magical power of the *shofar* is connected with its unconscious—thus its symbolic—significance. The *shofar* is also blown in order to awaken dormant powers—the divinity's unconscious forces—and prevail upon them to assist the believers who are blowing the *shofar* and, at that moment, need divine strength to help them in their hour of need. The sound of the *shofar* is meant to encourage them and give rise to hope, expiation, atonement, and redemption.

The *shofar* was used to summon a tribe or people to war or for defense, or to the coronation of a new king or leader. The *shofar* also was used in its symbolic female sense as a receptacle for the oil with which the leader was anointed. In this instance, the horn's symbolic attributes were combined, conferring upon the honored individual the symbols of power, might, and valor embodied in the horn upon his anointment with the oil stored in it.

The Bible refers to the *shofar* seventy times, including it in a list of musical instruments. "Music was still used as a magical basis to the rite. . . . The connection with magic disappeared, but it is to this day the basis of religious rites" (Finesinger 1931–32, col. 538). "The earliest musical instruments mentioned in the Bible include the *shofar,* the horn, trumpet, and drums. . . . These instruments are still shrouded in an atmosphere of magic. The sound of the *shofar* intermingles with the sound of thunder, the lightning, and the tumult of the events on Mount Sinai; it is a participant in bringing down the walls of Jericho, and it arouses fear and consternation. The *shofar* and the trumpets became holy instruments when their original symbolism was refined into spiritual significance" (ibid., col. 386).

The most interesting and meaningful use of the *shofar* is found in the biblical account of the divine revelation at Mount Sinai, where not only was the Torah given to the Israelites, but an initial attempt was made to forge the tribes into a homogenous unit under the authority of a single set of laws and rules—an attempt to change an assemblage of tribes into a community with a collective consciousness anchored in Abraham's act of the Binding as the father of the nation. The binding established the *shofar* as a symbol of an aggressive, bestial divinity, and of a balanced divine image that includes aspects of protector and supporter, makes demands, takes revenge, bears a grudge, yet abounds with mercy and compassion, atonement and redemption. All symbolic meaning of the *shofar* is concentrated in the revelation of Sinai. Symbolically, the *shofar* comes from the ram that substituted for Isaac. Its use in a situation that was created because of Isaac's individual redemption became a symbol for a group that united around the religious nucleus created at that time. This is why the Rosh Hashanah liturgy, accompanied by the sounding of the *shofar*, refers significantly to the Binding.

Additional parallels can be drawn between the binding and Sinai, the two most decisive events in Judaism. "On the third day, as morning dawned, there was thunder, and lightning, and a dense cloud upon the mountain, and a very loud blast of the horn; and all the people who were in the camp trembled. . . . The blare of the horn grew louder and louder. As Moses spoke, God answered him in thunder" (Exodus 19.16, 19).

What is striking here is the use of the archetypes of three, the mountain, and the morning. In Genesis, Abraham is given three days to prepare himself for the harshest and most traumatic task of his life. In Exodus, the people of Israel, as a community, are given three days to prepare to receive the word of God. God last appears before Abraham on Mount Moriah; now he appears before the nation on Mount Sinai. Both appearances are dramatic, numinous episodes that transform the private and public image of the divine. In Genesis, mercy and compassion are revealed as human elements within God and are liberated from the divinity's aggressiveness. Exodus brings forth the judge who promulgates laws and establishes rules for human existence. On Mount Moriah, Abraham sets out to fulfill the divine command in the morning, a symbol of inner illumination.

111

Similarly, at Mount Sinai, God is revealed to the nation in the morning. Moreover, the numinous ambience at the foot of Mount Sinai contains an allusion to magic ceremony through the use of tumult, thunder and lightning, the sound of the *shofar*, and the thick cloud on the mountain. These factors generate both fear and tension and tend to reduce the level of consciousness, and the *shofar* expresses the immediate presence of God.

In the Binding, the numinous sensation is created by Abraham's absolute, uncritical submission. At Mount Sinai, the nation promises "We will do and we will obey." The redemptive aspect of God is revealed. God has brought the Israelites out of slavery in Egypt, as he has redeemed Abraham from his religious frenzy and servitude to the image of the aggressive God concealed within himself.

Consequently, the *shofar* is also a symbol of God the redeemer, the savior, the rescuer. It is therefore only natural that there be an image of the Messiah blowing a great *shofar* to herald the advent of longed-for freedom from the sentence of death passed on human beings, just as the ram liberates Isaac from the death sentence passed on him by God, giving reason to hope for redemption and renewal.

This may explain why the *shofar*, as a symbol of hope and faith in the resurrection of the dead, is carved on tombstones. (Consider the *aggadah*, mentioned above, asserting that Isaac was in fact slaughtered, burnt on the altar, and then restored to life when the dew moistened his ashes.) As already noted, a magical ability to alter natural laws, open the heavens, and mobilize the positive forces of God for the assistance of humanity is projected onto the instrument; this is why the *shofar* is blown on the Days of Awe, when human deeds are weighed on the scales of the Almighty. The liturgy refers to the Binding as an argument in favor of absolving the people of Israel of their sins, and cites it in supplication for expiation.

An additional symbol of expiation accompanies the *shofar*-ram: the sending of the scapegoat ("And the goat shall bear upon him all their iniquities unto a land which is cut off; and he shall let go the goat in the wilderness"—Lev. 16.22). The scapegoat is the substitute victim for the collective sins of the people of Israel. *Goat* is defined in the *Even-Shoshan Hebrew Dictionary* (1969) as "a designation for one of the hirsute wild animals which early idol worshippers considered to have the strength of the gods." In the pagan context, we have already noted the linguistic connection between *el* (God), *elil* (idol or false god), and *eyal* (ram). The sacrifice of the scapegoat thus also symbolizes the human release from aggression, regressiveness, and image of the divinity. As we understand it, it also symbolizes purging the vestiges of paganism.

Thus the *shofar* is a symbol of the unceasing conflict among the positive and the negative aspects, the pagan regressive and aggressive aspects of God or selfhood, as well as the human aspect of grace and compassion, and hope for redemption. People are freed of their aggressive urges when the divinity is incorporated in selfhood, where the compassion and loving-kindness within them are accessible.

In Jewish tradition the *shofar* recalls human self-sacrifice for God; a private individual experience turns into a collective symbol. The blowing of the *shofar* evokes memories of the awesome and numinous episode of the Binding, when, as Isaac lies bound on the altar, suspended between life and death, the ram appears. The sudden shift from immediate, threatened death to life that was experienced by Isaac and Abraham is called, in Jungian terminology, enantiodromia—an outburst of the opposite, unconscious side. During a situation in which all personal energies are directed to one specific channel, an opposite unconscious content suddenly penetrates consciousness. Just as Isaac is resigned to death, the ram materializes as a symbol of life. The animal is his savior—the ram will die instead, and Isaac is condemned to life that is taken from the beast. Thus the *shofar* symbolizes the transition from death to life: it illustrates the archetype of regeneration—and re-creation, as with the seasons of the year or the rising of the sun after its "death" in the night. After the death of the old year, a new year is born. The use of the *shofar* in the rituals of Rosh Hashanah may be an echo, a reminder, of this archetype as much as a way of symbolizing the binding itself. For the believer, the sounding of the *shofar* signals a new lease on life, atonement, and forgiveness for sins. The believer's point of departure is the transgressions listed in the liturgy, for which he must be punished. The sounding of the *shofar* provides the believer with the magic strength (to which he would not admit) to transform his fate through divine forgiveness, thereby transforming himself and, concomitantly, objective reality.

One example of the *shofar* as a living symbol in the collective consciousness of every Jew is the spontaneous blowing of the *shofar* at the Western Wall when the Old City of Jerusalem was captured from Jordan during the Six-Day War. In the moments of human excitement connected to numinous episodes, a religious symbol that dwells within the nation's collective consciousness is adapted to a secular situation, infusing the people involved with a sense of spiritual elevation and psychic exaltation.

The *shofar*, symbolizing at once the victim, the aggressor, and the forfeiting of aggression, as well as hope, expiation, regeneration, and revival, was a fitting symbol for that situation, after the long period of waiting, fear, anxiety, apprehension, and "impotence" in face of a possible extinction of Israel. The blowing of the *shofar* expresses relief and salvation; it is a manifestation of nationality, a living symbol linking past and present.

The symbolic attributes of the *shofar*, as modified, refined, and elaborated over the generations, have been subject to the laws of human development, the constant interaction between the conscious and unconscious mind. Lest we forget, the unconscious is both a source of human creativity (the Hebrew for *instinct, yetser*, is related to *creation, yetsira*) and the source of the shadow. Both are characterized by alternating advance and retreat as they pursue the trend toward human perfection. The Self and the ego, the active and the passive, the father and the son, are concurrently the sacrificer and the sacrifice. This is a paradox of the reality within which we live. The individuation process, on the personal and the collective levels, is not divorced from the personal ego. Both, in constant movement, nurture each other, modifying each other in unceasing flux between the poles of the personality—the personal and the transpersonal.

Abraham, as a human symbol, an archetype, embraces and envelops Isaac, and is himself embraced by the wider sphere of God, of the transpersonal selfhood. The wider sphere of the divine selfhood symbolizes both the personal and the collective, the personal being in the center of the collective, both affecting each other reciprocally and unceasingly.

Each individual is both a personal, private selfhood and an archetypal collective being, thus simultaneously the sacrificer and the sacrifice. Individuation aims to achieve the ability to make the distinction and become conscious of the existence of this dynamic. As a result of the consciousness acquired painfully and through unlimited suffering, a person is liberated from the domination of instincts and impulses. He is not blindly swept to the Binding like

114

Isaac, nor does he sacrifice in an uncontrolled frenzy like Abraham. He acts on the basis of consciousness of the opposing poles within his personality, avoiding domination by an archetypal idea originating in a myth or mythology that dictates his actions. He is able to distinguish and choose among his inner attributes, and to act after due reflection and in compliance with ethical criteria that have evolved within him in the course of his personal development.

Twelve

The Aftermath

Before the Binding, the destructive and murderous facet of Abraham's personality is projected onto the deity, taking the form of a demand to offer Isaac as a sacrifice. Abraham has not yet become aware that the voice of God emanates from within himself. His violent struggle with his shadow is a human regression to the level of being on which primal urges dominate the conscious personality.

The voice rising from the Self may be so intense that it overwhelms the ego, which finds itself unable to criticize or examine the Self's pernicious demands. The ego loses conscious control and submits to the violence of the command. At this moment, the ego becomes the victim of the Self's destructive energy.

Jung defines regression as a retreat, an attempt to reinvigorate and refresh the personality through an encounter and attachment with the father- or god-figure, and, consequently, as an action in which the Self participates. This action leads inexorably to the disintegration of the ego in its previous form and, consequently, to the attenuation of the tension and emotions of the previous way of life.

After the Binding, Abraham returns to ordinary life, to a healthy routine free of tension and overt emotional turmoil. He has no further encounters with the deity-Self that would create numinous experiences and emotions that arouse the Self and challenge the world order. Never again does Abraham experience the suspense and anticipation of encounters with the deity and Self-generated dictates. Abraham reaches the climax of his life at the Binding.

In *Symbols of Transformation*, Jung writes: "That the highest summit of life can be expressed through the symbolism of death is a

117

well-known fact, for any growing beyond oneself means death"
(1956, par. 432). At the Binding, Abraham nearly leaves the boundaries of himself. On the verge of death he himself is deterred by the
command of the angel, the emissary of the merciful aspect of the
deity. Death is hovering in the air. Its victim, however, is neither
Abraham nor Isaac but Sarah.

Jung adds: "The separation of the son from the mother signifies
man's leavetaking from animal unconsciousness" (1956, par. 415).
Isaac must separate from his mother in order to acquire self-aware-
ness, and to fulfill the role destined for him as the second patriarch
and the performer of the tasks and duties thrust upon him by virtue
of his father's devotional awareness. Abraham must part with the
image of the violent deity and the vestiges of his pre-Binding world,
which includes the principle of the anima as embodied in Sarah. The
Binding must end with death—death not only as the absence of the
violent, animal unconsciousness symbolized by the sacrifice of the
ram, but death as the death of a person.

The idea of death, however, contains the promise of rebirth:
the birth of a consciousness that leads to insight of the most profound kind, an insight that probes all the wondrous, awesome elements at work within the human psyche, including the violence of
the unconscious dynamic that exists within it. Sarah, Abraham's wife,
is a living symbol of his inner spiritual principle, the anima. With this
principle finally internalized, the woman herself is no longer necessary. Because Sarah is a tool in Abraham's spiritual evolution, her
role has come to an end.

The connection between the Binding and Sarah's death is natural and logical, not only because of the juxtaposition of chapters 22
and 23 but also because of their content. "He came from Mount
Moriah and Sarah died of this sorrow. This is why the account of the
Binding is immediately followed by that of the life of Sarah"
(*Midrash Genesis Rabbah*). The Sages also stressed the substantive
and causal linkage between the two chapters. One dictum states that
Sarah died of anguish when Satan told her of the horror that Abraham had perpetrated on his son; another explains that she died of
joy when told that her son had been spared. In either case she suc-
cumbs, paying the price for the consciousness that Abraham and
Isaac attained at the Binding. With the achievement of consciousness, death came into the world, because of the sin of Adam and
Eve—eating the fruit from the tree of knowledge in the Garden of

Eden. Right after the scene of the Binding, Abraham comes to bury his dead. He laments Sarah, mourns for her, and attends to the burial arrangements. The voice of Isaac is not heard. Abraham's encampment is situated in Qiryat Arba' (Hebron) at this time, and it is here that he must dig the first grave in the Promised Land, dissociating himself symbolically from his previous identity and his relationship with the pagan world from which he and Sarah came.

Despite his bereavement and pain on the death of his wife, Abraham retains one of his most important personality traits, pragmatism. Instead of relying on the divine promise that the land of Canaan is all his, he seeks to purchase the burial plot from its owner, Ephron the Hittite. With outstanding diplomatic panache, Abraham negotiates in a fashion reminiscent of typical Oriental bargaining. What follows is a ritual associated with the commercial tradition of this milieu, in which each side glorifies and extols the other with sublime etiquette, and an ostensible diminishing of his own "business ego." In this manner, Abraham acquires the Cave of the Makhpela and its appurtenances for a price that evidently far exceeds its actual value.

After Sarah's burial, with the anima principle internalized and assimilated into Abraham's personality, the biblical account summarizes the process of Abraham's individuation in the follow verse: "And the Lord had blessed Abraham in all things" (Gen. 24.1). In terms of Jungian psychology, Abraham has achieved self-fulfillment. His ego and the Self interact, permitting a life of greater meaning, depth, and harmony among all parts of the psyche, within the constraints of his society and culture. Individuation occurs not in a vacuum but relative to the collective truths of society, even if one rebels against them—truths, not beliefs, which generate new life patterns and ideals, culture and ways of life, and beliefs and opinions, on social and individual levels. On the collective level, Abraham adapts and adjusts to Canaanite social norms, as we have seen. On the personal level, he adjusts by realizing and acknowledging that he is a unique person but not superhuman. Abraham, who nearly transcended the human plane, attains a humility commensurate with his experiences and his attitude toward his inner world, his God, and the outside world. The ego gives of itself, sacrifices all it can to the Self-deity, and receives in return a psychologically balanced, whole psyche. It is this that allows the ego and the Self to conduct an ongoing, fruitful dialogue.

The totality of Abraham's conscious personality enables him to accept the death of his wife, who played an active role in his development, in her additional function as the deity's spokesperson. "Whatever Sarah tells you, do as she says" (Gen. 21.12), says the deity-inner voice, even if her instructions are inconsistent with or even contrary to his ethical perception. Sarah represents a major segment of Abraham's personality, the anima, one of the functions of which is to make the psyche better able to absorb irrational emotions. Upon her death, Abraham acquires a sudden and wholesome awareness of the proximity of his own death and mortality.

Rashi's commentary on Genesis 24.1 applies to our thesis. He likens the word *ba-kol* (in all things) to *ben* (son). Each Hebrew letter has a numerical value, thus permitting *gematriya*—interpretation of names and words. The numerical value of *kol* is fifty: twenty for *kaf* plus thirty for *lamed*. Because the letter *nun* bears the value of fifty, one may substitute *nun* for *kol*. Hence *ba-kol* becomes *ben*. Abraham's wealth, his "all things," is his son, through whom he is blessed. Isaac is both Abraham's wealth and the extension of his being, the physical expression that symbolizes, with his body, Abraham's most exalted and terrifying numinous experience. Isaac is the physical manifestation of Abraham's psychological self-fulfillment, and he is the device by which Abraham disseminates his internal truth as a collective one on the religious, philosophical, and ethical levels.

Here we propose an additional remark in the spirit of Rashi's commentary. *Gematriya* allows one to manipulate the position of letters in a word and thereby attain a new meaning. *Kol* equals *lekh* (the command *go*), recalling the first command that Abraham heard: "Go forth" (Gen. 21.1). To go forth toward self-fulfillment is the first step in the process of individuation. This process is now completed; the cycle of Abraham's experiences is completed and refined in his son, Isaac. Abraham's conscious life begins with *lekh* and, because the *ben* exists, also ends with *lekh*.

Abraham's struggle with himself and his God has come to an end. From now on, he must work through his experiences, in which tremendous psychic energy has been invested. He must digest them and descend from the heights of his sense of identification with the deity, returning to the plane of the human, the simple, to Abraham the mortal man. This may explain why Abraham no longer hears the inner voice and no longer experiences the numinous presence of the deity, instead drawing strength from the well of memories.

Isaac is the essence and the inevitable outcome of Abraham's being. Had Abraham failed to perfect himself, Isaac would not have come into existence. Therefore, acting from a sense of responsibility to the ego, to the self-deity, and to his future, sensing that time is short and death imminent, Abraham decides to marry off his son. He does not entrust Isaac with the responsibility or the right to choose a wife of his liking. It stands to reason that a patriarch who selects his children's marriage partners is merely following the custom of the time. Abraham's behavior, however, denies Isaac the right to agree or disagree with the proposed choice. Rebecca, by contrast, is given this privilege: "Let us call the girl and ask for her reply" (Gen. 24.57).

It is Abraham who makes this decision for Isaac, wielding exclusive authority over his son's life. This man, who in middle age left his birthplace and ventured into the unknown to choose a new life, this innovator and revolutionary in his tenets and beliefs, becomes in old age a traditional conservative who reverts to the tried-and-true formula of arranged marriages within the family. Instinctively driven to preserve and safeguard the family energy, he returns to his roots.

The Abraham shown to us at this point in the biblical account is an autocrat who values the well-being of his son, *as he understands it*, over any other consideration, even ruling out the possibility of consulting with Isaac. This behavior is better suited to Sarah than to Abraham. Because Abraham brought life into being and nearly took it away, he is the sole master of Isaac's life. His attitude is reminiscent of that of a sovereign toward a subject without rights. There is no dialogue between Abraham and Isaac. Abraham acts; Isaac is acted upon. The person whom Abraham trusts, with whom he chooses to consult and share his vacillations, is the servant Eliezer, not Isaac.

Eliezer symbolizes the part of Abraham's psyche that submits to the ego and follows its dictates. Consequently, the dictates of Abraham's inner voice apply to him, too. The God of Abraham is the God of Eliezer. It is Abraham's inner voice that guides Eliezer as he sets out to fulfill his mission, bearing "all the bounty of his master" (Gen. 24.10). The expression "all the bounty" not only signifies the material bounty, an ostentatious display of Abraham's wealth, but also symbolizes his inner wealth, the psychic strength and the faith with which he is graced. "O Lord, God of my master Abraham, grant me good fortune this day . . ." (Gen. 24.12), Eliezer prays, convinced that his master has magic, miracle-working powers that are called "the God of Abraham." Eliezer is utterly dominated by the psychic might that he attributes to Abraham, and begs these forces to help him find the wife best suited to Isaac. The name *Eliezer* is composed of two words, *eli* and *'ezer*, which together mean "my God is my help"—a suitable name for Abraham's servant, whom God does in fact help by producing a suitable young woman through a synchronistic chain of events. Rabbinical sources also describe Eliezer as an active extension of Abraham's psyche, to the extent of both men having similar facial features (Ginzberg 1954). It is this man who is empowered to select the woman who will enter Abraham's household as Isaac's wife.

Abraham does not regard Canaanite women as suitable marriage partners, and he orders Eliezer to vow "not [to] take a wife for my son from the daughters of the Canaanites among whom I dwell" (Gen. 24.3). This statement reflects Abraham's scorn and contempt for the local population. Perhaps their customs are alien to him; perhaps, too, he believes himself culturally superior as the product of a different and more developed civilization, that of Ur of the Chaldees, the Sumerian capital that functioned as the cultural and political center of the tribes of the area. Abraham's aversion to his neighbors is reflected in the intensity of his prohibition to Eliezer against Isaac's taking a Canaanite wife: "And I will make you swear by the Lord, the God of heaven and the God of the earth" (Gen. 24.3). Only an oath of the utmost gravity, an absolute and irrevocable taboo, would invoke heaven and earth as witnesses.

According to the dominant view of the time—one that is still encountered in various societies today—marriage is a matter for the entire family. The family's strength and honor are measured by its economic wealth, the number of its members, and its kinship relations with families of equal or superior status within the clan. It was therefore natural that a family would attempt to preserve and enhance its strength by creating suitable marriages, because marriage outside the tribe would dilute and therefore diminish the family strength. Abraham has no relatives in Canaan. Lot and his family were expelled from the family circle and assimilated into the local population. Therefore, to choose a wife for Isaac, Eliezer must return to Mesopotamia, to the city of Nahor, Abraham's birthplace, where the patriarch's next of kin live. Abraham instinctively acts as a traditional conservative and returns to his origins, following the dictum: "Better a small portion of one's own than a large portion of others'."

Abraham then gives Eliezer a further stipulation: "On no account must you take my son back there!" (Gen. 24.6). Abraham is terrified by the possibility of Isaac's return to the pagan world that he had abandoned. Were this to happen, the entire divine promise would be annulled. The result would be a regression from conscious life into the lowly recesses of the unconscious world that precedes the command "Go forth"; it would nullify and obfuscate Abraham's spiritual and psychological achievements. Even though he regards Isaac as an extension of his own being and self, he does not trust his son's discretion and judgment.

The wife-to-be must abandon her world and home, and go with Eliezer. Eliezer raises the following objection: "What if the woman does not consent to follow me to this land?" (Gen. 24.5), to which Abraham answers: "You shall then be clean of this oath" (Gen. 24.8). Nevertheless, Abraham believes that "[God] will send His angel before you" (Gen. 24.7). Abraham's trust in divine assistance originates in his view of God as an inner personal entity, not only as an all-embracing and generally valid substance. God is an active source in Abraham's innermost psyche—the voice of his inner Self, as we have termed it. However, this is also the source of the constraints to his ability. Despite his personal trust in a force that guides and directs him in his actions, the possibility exists that God is not omnipotent and that his promise is limited to his relationship with Abraham only.

Rebecca meets all of Abraham's stipulations to Eliezer. The granddaughter of Abraham's brother, she displays free will and uncommon courage by following a stranger to an unknown land, in order to marry a man she has never seen. One cannot disregard the parallelism of Rebecca's voyage into the unknown and Abraham's trek to "the land that I will show you" (Gen. 12.1). The place where the divine command leads is nameless, totally anonymous. Nevertheless, out of absolute trust in the voice that speaks to him, Abraham goes. The family that sired a child who shatters conventions, who rebels, who follows the dictates of his heart, and who creates a new world for himself, has also produced a daughter who is prepared to abandon her family and a safe, stable home, in order to walk an unknown path. The spirit of "Go forth" hovers over Rebecca who, like Abraham, answers to no one but herself and decides her own fate. Rebecca, by virtue of a synchronistic sequence of events that symbolizes the hand of fate or divine action, achieves her goal: self-fulfillment. Thus, she is a female reflection of Abraham.

It is true that Rebecca's going forth is not motivated by an inner dictate that emanates from her Self and is identified as the voice of God. Instead, she is driven by an instinctive awareness that this path will lead her to herself and enable her to fulfill her feminine personality.

Rebecca is led to Sarah's tent, where she is entrusted with her mission: "And he took Rebecca as his wife. Isaac loved her, and thus found comfort after his mother's death" (Gen. 24.67). Abraham has provided Isaac with an object for his love and his projections: a wife, a steadfast, strong, and wise anchor on which he can lean all his life. With this, Abraham's mission is completed.

It is true, at least according to the order of events in the biblical account, that Abraham remarries after the marriage of his son. This event, however, has no profound inner meaning. It leads neither to tumultuous ordeals nor to heartbreak. Abraham eventually dismisses the offspring of this marriage with no pangs of conscience. His treatment of these sons illuminates a previously encountered facet of his personality: the dispassionate, coldly calculating Abraham whose loyalties are limited to one person only—Isaac, the extension and embodiment of his own life and self. Before his death, he liberates Isaac from any encumbrance that these offspring may cause him. He believes his son will need support and assistance even after his death.

Abraham passes away at a ripe old age. Isaac and Ishmael bury him in the family tomb at the Cave of Makhpela alongside Sarah, his only meaningful wife. Abraham dies without hearing the divine voice again. After the Binding, he no longer has room for further numinous experiences, having already experienced the greatest of them all.

Thirteen

The Echo of the Binding
in Contemporary Israeli Prose and Poetry

Abraham's individuation, of which the Binding is the dramatic and cruel climax, is relevant for today, the experience being the archetype of sacrifice. This experience is gained, over the years and across the generations, by individuals and peoples everywhere, in varying degrees of intensity. However, only for the Jewish people has the archetype of sacrifice become both a private and personal, as well as a national and public experience, in both religious rite and daily life. For this reason, we have chosen to examine the work of five contemporary Israeli writers to see how the experience of the binding of Isaac is reflected in our generation—a generation on which the Holocaust and various national conflicts have cast their shadows.

Jung's definitions of the archetype are dispersed throughout his writings, his work having, in effect, being expanded and developed over the years; thus, a plethora of complementary definitions has been added to the basic nuclear idea. The archetype is a collective image with independent energy and power, which speaks in images and is capable of influencing people and directing their actions. "The collective unconscious represents the stock of primordial images which everybody brings with him as his human birthright, the sum total of inborn forms, peculiar to the instincts" (Jung 1956, par. 631). Together with the collective unconscious, the personal unconscious contains the memory, repressions, images, and projections of the individual's personal psychic life. The influence of the archetype is present and perceived to varying degrees in all the individual's actions and throughout their life, consciously or otherwise.

The archetype is revealed, as frequently shown, in early images, its content charged with energy and present within the unconscious. The artistic creator is the closest to such content, from which creativity is derived and elaborated. Because the artist is highly sensitive, discerning and attentive to what takes place in their innermost mind and in their surroundings, the individual processes experiences through a personal perspective. Thus it is obvious why, in certain situations of pressure created by the environment and contemporary events, archetypal, symbolic pictures and patterns emanate from within her.

In situations of extreme pressure such as disasters and wars, which overwhelm us and influence the national mood and state of mind, the ancient image of the binding recurs. This image originates in the archetype of sacrifice; it has become coupled with the attributes and significance attached to it throughout the generations. Jung notes that archetypes are not only records of typical experiences that keep recurring, but—as empirical experience shows—they also act forcefully or tendentiously to repeat such experiences (1953, par. 109). The repetition of these experiences is endowed with the profound psychological significance of cognition and consciousness of personal destiny as a vital and inseparable part of human destiny, of the individual's liberation from the total control of the ego. The process leads to humility as well as to the integration of archetypal attributes in the personality, and it facilitates the use of certain cultural symbols in interpersonal communication. An archetype enables expression through a symbol largely understood in the cultural context in which the individual lives and acts.

The artist expresses an archetypal experience through his personal mirror, which, through sound, word, or form, triggers in the reader, the viewer, or the listener a charge of dynamic archetypal attributes deep within the psyche. In this manner, a numinous and therefore cathartic experience comes about. "The archetype . . . has a characteristically numinous effect" (1956, par. 225). According to the dictionary definition, catharsis is a separation and purification from desires and appetites, from affects and internal tensions, through identification and involvement in the experience displayed. (The concept of catharsis is borrowed from the Aristotelian vocabulary attached to the experience of viewing a theatrical depiction, and has been included in the conceptual lexicon of psychology.) The artist involves the listener, reader, or viewer in a general and group experience, so that those who respond to the art do not remain isolated with their experiential burden. The audience experiences and participates in the archetype that is activated, that is given expression, and that speaks in comprehensible symbols and pictures. In this instance, the archetype operates in the polarizing dynamics of the episode of the Binding, our present context. This incessant oscillation of thesis and antithesis together and separately composes the synthesis of overall life. They are the paradox of the divinity and of human reality; they represent the ceaseless striving for individuation.

Since the Bible became the cultural inheritance of the Western world, many of the world's outstanding artists have dealt with the motif of the Binding. (The archetype of the sacrifice was also of concern in classical Greece, in India, and, indeed, throughout the ancient world.) Human sacrifice is an internal litmus test for any artist who is attempting to comprehend the terrible significance of all sacrifices.

Many cultural and religious changes have taken place in the course of history with regard to the meaning of sacrifice. It was burdened with interpretations and justifications, and considerable feeling was projected onto it. Each of the writers we have chosen—completely at random, if truth be told, on the basis of personal preference alone—appropriates one of the participants in the Binding as a symbol of particular significance. Therefore, each artist with his own interpretation is directed by his weltanschauung, his religion, his personal situation, and the influence of his society. The participant in the story "speaks" to him and triggers his artistic instinct—every detail, both animate and inanimate, excites his imagination. The account of the Binding occasionally transcends the personal reference of the individual, entering into a unconventional conception of the world and the divinity, as in the following passage by S. Yizhar:

> I hate Abraham our Forefather, on his way to sacrifice Isaac. What is his merit over that of Isaac? Let him bind himself. I hate the God Who sent him to carry out the Binding and closed his every path, save that leading to the Binding. I hate the fact that Isaac is merely an object for experimentation: an experiment between Abraham and his God. I hate this proof of love. This demand to prove love. God's self-sanctification in the Binding of Isaac. I hate to be a killer of children as a test of love! To summon strength and to

intervene and to take away life in order to prove something in a struggle. And because the world has become deaf and has not risen up and cried: scoundrels, why must the children die? I hate the necessity to achieve something at the cost of destruction or annihilation, or torment, or force. I doubt that it has any value—that which is achieved only through destruction. It is a more beautiful thing to give up, to shrug one's shoulders and continue on one's way—than to fight, to grab. I hate fighting more than anything. It is utterly contemptible. And I sit here and wait for murder, killing, destruction, and dispel all my strength, my nerves, my muscle and my mind—for the last moment when I, too, according to my strength, shall be able to spring and catch my prey, to save my life by preying in turn, biting and stabbing at the throat. And there is no earthly way out. This is how the world is built. This is how life is built. This is how it is built. It is decreed. One cannot even flee. If you are not prepared to die and to kill—there will be no good in the world. No justice, no love, no beauty. All of these—only through you. If you are not prepared to offer up your life, to leap into the fire, to go forth to battle and to kill cleverly, aggressively, with much slaughter—there will be no world and no life; all will be utter chaos. This is how the world is built. This is its right order. And I, myself, have no other personal way than to take part. (1967)

Yizhar protests all killing. He is against the divine image that is able to confront people and demand human sacrifice, and against people who are capable of surrendering to this image. He expands the concept of the Binding of the individual to a public that is condemned to a cycle of war and killing, a way of life based on war and blood, with nothing to be done other than making a private, personal protest, releasing a cry to the heavens. Yizhar aspires to a divine image that has no need for unceasing human sacrifice. He does, however, acknowledge that the world is as ambivalent as its God. He views the Binding as an event that forces one to confront the unbearable pain inflicted by the loss of human life.

Yizhar protests against the divinity with an intensity that shakes one to the depths of the soul: the bitter cry of "I hate God." He protests the traditional view of Abraham as the "Knight of Faith," as Kierkegaard put it. However, he also acquiesces to the bitter realities and cruel laws that apply to the world in which he lives and to which he must submit.

To Amir Gilboa (1963), the Binding is a manifestation of the helplessness that comes from personal experience and permeates the collective domain. For him, it is a symbol of the terror of the Holocaust. Thus he writes:

ISAAC

In the morning the sun journeyed in the forest.
Together with me and with father.
My right hand in his left.

Like the flash of the blade among the trees.
And I so fearful, so afraid of blood on the leaves.

Father, father, quick, save Isaac.
Let no one be absent from the noontime meal.

I am the one who is slaughtered, my son.
And my blood is already on the leaves.
And father—his voice is choked.
And his face white.

And I wanted to scream, palpitating, disbelieving.
And tore my eyes open.
And woke up.
And there was a right hand bloodless.

This is a situation of utter helplessness, a personal experience of the child Isaac, describing the death of his father, which we interpret as the death of innocent faith. Gilboa's Isaac is not the Isaac of the Bible; neither is the father the biblical Abraham, who carries out the sacrifice. Gilboa does not raise his voice in protest against God; he does not address God at all. His subject is the dead father, a symbol of the God who has disappointed the child Isaac, leaving him helpless in the face of unnamed evil.

The shift of the setting of the Binding from the mountain to the forest translocates the altar to a European landscape—the poet's allusion to the Holocaust. Thus Gilboa has transformed the individual's personal experience into the collective experience of a people. In this way, Gilboa keeps the Binding within the domain of the here and now. Does this imply that private or public bindings are experiences forced upon human beings by their daily reality?

There follows an unsuccessful attempt at self-delusion, suggesting that the Binding is merely a nightmare. "And the right hand was bloodless." Humanity is powerless against the decree of the Binding, utterly helpless in the face of the flashing knife of the slaughterer. There is no salvation, no redemption.

Gilboa's poem is structured in a quasi-sonnet form—fourteen lines plus one that summarizes and draws conclusions. The poem abounds with archetypes, which, although interesting, are not dealt with here, since our focus is the motif of the Binding only.

Whereas Gilboa sets his poem in a European landscape, Mati Meged (1973) writes about the war-torn reality of modern Israel, in which father and son alike become offerings sacrificed in episodes reminiscent of the Binding—an archetypal situation, occurring again and again:

THE BINDING

And when again I went to the Binding
(Not on foot, not riding on a donkey.
Trapped in the belly of a steel monster)—
My father's warm hand
Did not grasp mine.
I did not ask: and where is the lamb for the offering?
And there was no one to reply to my question.

Nor was there an angel
To stop the knife.

Only I on my own—
The father and the son.

And there is no spirit
To sanctify with my blood
The altar of basalt stones.

Behind me remains:
A burnt-out cannon barrel,
Rising, finger accusing
To the alien, smoke-filled skies,
Wiping out all trace
Of my life and death.

For but a few more moments shall I still hear
Through the clouds
The voice of an old sinner
Laughing at my annihilation.

Meged stresses the loneliness of a person bound in the world of modern warfare. No questions are asked, no replies proffered. The divinity has hidden its face. Humanity is on its own: people make sacrifices and are themselves sacrificed. Here Meged takes the view of Abraham and Isaac as a single victim. But the sacrifice of victims is for naught. The accusing finger, protesting to the divinity the loss of life and the squandering of the human dream, is itself the weapon of destruction.

Meged's poem presents a divinity mocking those who dream, who make sacrifices, as well as the sacrifices themselves, thus belittling the value of human life. His God is a god of wanton evil. The emphasis is on humanity's dissociation from a merciless God ("Nor was there an angel to stop the knife"). Responsibility for this painful separation is assigned to the divinity, who is presented as a sinner, a doer of injustice, shameless and cynical. The hero of this poem is the gun-barrel—the knife—which protests against people and their God.

The third poet, Ayin Hillel (1973), transposes the Binding to a cold, alienated dream world, to a dialogue between a Jew and the moon—his unconscious. "A land of desert sand" stands in contrast to the biblical land of Moriah. The poet contrasts meanings, using words derived from a single root to create a milieu of opposites, of pressure and tension. The Hebrew *Eretz holat midbar* may be construed either as a sandy desert (*midbar hol*) or a sickly desert (*midbar holeh*); similarly, the change of one vowel, from *o* to *i*, yields lime (*sid*), which causes whitening, and a secret (*sod*) of the desert. From the dunes (*holot*), or from the ailments (*holaim*), arises the persona of the victim, an anonymous soldier boy, identified as the beloved son mounting the altar. But there is no redeemer, no ram, no hope, no consolation, only universal suffering. The movement of the moon, "shrouded in clouds," expresses shame for the pain caused. Of the luminaries in the heavens, the moon symbolizes the suffering that engulfs the entire universe, a cosmic pain for the fate of humanity.

The ram is not present here. However, by using the biblical

expression "a man of Israel" for the individual Jew, the poet trans-
ports the victim into the collective domain of the entire people of
Israel. Hillel's poem does not refer to the God who demands the
sacrifice. Rather, the work alludes to God's dissociation from human
reality, as a result of which humanity is in the desert—a hostile terrain symbolizing isolation and sickness.

No Ram in His Stead

Far away in a land of desert sand
A lofty moon blazes
And a man of Israel stands at a window
Lifting his eyes to the moon.

What do you see down there,
Moon, what do you see?

As lime makes the moon pale, so
The secret of the desert beneath it.

O speak, moon, do not fear,
Be the sight as it may be!

There, at the end of the desert, I see
A soldier boy who looks to be asleep
There, with his face in the sand.

O speak, moon, do you recognize
This boy, O this boy?
For I shall say what I see:
Indeed, "Thy son, thine only son, whom thou lovest" is here.
And there is no ram in the thicket in his stead.
Spake the moon and shrouded itself in a cloud.

And the man of Israel shrouded his face.

The poet Haim Gouri (1966) retells the account of the Binding
almost as it appears in the Bible, emphasizing the human situations
that are absent from the laconic biblical story. The poem contains a
particularly damning wordless accusation by Isaac of his father for
having submitted to God's inhuman demand that he be sacrificed,
and of the father's shame for having submitted to this cruel com-

mand ("The child . . . saw his father's back"). The father, the object of the child's trust in the world, cannot look into his son's accusing eyes—eyes that do not question, for the answers are given.

BEQUEST

The ram came last.
And Abraham knew not that he
Was answering the child's question,
His first-born, in the eve of his day.

He elevated his head back.
When he saw he was not having a dream
And the angel was there
The knife fell from his hand.

The child, released from his fetters,
Saw his father's back.

As narrated, Isaac was not offered up.
He lived a long life,
Lived a good life, until his eye dimmed.

But he bequeathed that hour to his descendants.
They are born
With the sacrificial knife in their hearts.

God ultimately provides salvation from immediate death, but the terror of death remains engraved in the boy's heart. This is the "fear of Isaac" (Hebrew, *pahad yitzhak*, Genesis 31.42), an existential state, the fear of annihilation and destruction. The poet then shifts to the collective domain of the fate of the people of Israel, for whom the terror of death is combined with the vision of salvation symbolized by the ram. However, Gouri's concluding section may also be construed as the everlasting anguish of the father, the son, or both, who have been disillusioned and whose trust has been breached. They endure the fear, the terrible, helpless disappointment that Isaac bequeaths to all his descendants—the memory of the single experience that shaped the fate of an entire people, the national trauma, relived over and again by the people of Israel: "They are born/ With the sacrificial knife in their hearts."

Fourteen

Kierkegaard, Jung, and A. I. Kook on Faith

We would be remiss if we concluded this book without referring to one of the greatest works on Abraham: Soren Kierkegaard's *Fear and Trembling* (1909). Abraham's life, the way he deals with his inner world as it evolves on the path to an internal truth imposed by the negation of the pagan world in which he previously lived, and the creation of different behavioral patterns and powers derived from a new set of human values (what we have called, in Jungian terms, the process of individuation) are themes that have been considered by many thinkers, of whom Kierkegaard is perhaps the greatest.

Kierkegaard's philosophical-emotional weltanschauung was completely different from ours. Anyone who reads his philosophical essay, brief in length but great in significance, cannot but sense and be moved by the intensity of feelings he invested in it, and must inevitably be overwhelmed by his style and his lyrical form of expression. His outlook may be defined in general terms as religious existentialism. Kierkegaard is considered the father of existentialism, a philosophical system in which existence transcends thought.

Kierkegaard calls Abraham the "Knight of Faith." "Knight" evokes strength, heroism, forcefulness, and audacity. The knight embodies all these and acts according to predetermined criteria. When coupled with the concept of faith, religious intensity is combined with strength. This title does indeed fit Abraham. As Kierkegaard indicates, Abraham believes in God because of God's paradoxical nature. With respect to God, everything is possible. Faith, therefore, is an existential paradox. Since God is omnipotent, all-embracing, all-encompassing—point and counterpoint—he is a paradox. Faith is a miracle. Abraham's greatness lies in his ability to make the leap of faith, to transcend thought. Faith is a lust in which all aspects of human life are unified. Thus the yearning for faith nullifies human logic. In the account of the Binding, therefore, teleological ethics are negated and suspended: Abraham is a unique individual, transcending the generality of human beings.

God demands absolute love. As Kierkegaard expresses it, Abraham knows that God would not demand Isaac as a sacrifice had he been willing to sacrifice him, or had he not loved him limitlessly. Through his faith in a God for whom everything is possible, Abraham wins Isaac rather than renouncing him. Thus Abraham crosses the boundaries of the tragic hero who operates within the parameters of the ethical and the overt. He functions on a different level altogether. Every individual is capable of faith, but not of doing what Abraham does. His purpose (*telos*) is loftier. God's will (the Binding) becomes his own. (Interestingly, the *aggadah* assigns Satan the task of thwarting the realization of God's will.)

Kierkegaard's essay does not attempt to examine the psychic and psychological processes that occur within the human mind, either of the "Knight of Faith" or anyone else, when faced with the terrible dilemma of having to choose between two loves. Neither struggle nor vacillation, but only complete submission is possible, because the will of God is the will of Abraham, who is one with God. There is no reference to human conflict. Abraham has left the human domain.

In contrast with Kierkegaard's religious-existential approach, Jung's weltanschauung is symbolic and existential. In the Jungian view, Abraham must be regarded as the symbol of an inward struggle, in which God and his commands are components of Abraham's psyche. Jung regards faith and the function of religion as psychic imperatives that exist in all human beings, on one level or another. Jung writes: "When, therefore, we make use of the concept of a God, we are simply formulating a definite psychological fact; namely, the independence and sovereignty of certain psychic contents that express themselves by their power to thwart our will, to obsess our consciousness, and to influence our moods and actions" (1953, par. 400).

Jung is aware of the existence of a supreme psychological force that must be taken into account, even as its demands must be understood and applied. However, he does not define it as a supreme religious force that must be believed in and accepted unreservedly.

Kierkegaard regards faith as "that paradox by which the individual (the believer, Abraham) as an individual transcends the generality and whose justification stands in his stead relative to the generality. He is not subject to the laws of the generality, being above them" (1909). In Jungian psychological terms, when Abraham carries out God's will, which has become his, he enters a phase of psychological "inflation"—the stage at which the individual loses his humanity. Only then, being caught up in and controlled by the archetype of belief, is the person able to act against human nature. According to Kierkegaard, Abraham transcends the individual and the general, attaining the status of an archetypal symbol as described by Jung.

A person who makes a paradoxical submission to a paradoxical demand by God has achieved an inevitable paradox: all human ethical conventions are negated, as they have no validity for God, who is beyond human definition. Ultimately, the person who submits in this way arrives at the negation of God himself. The paradox of God's reality is that God embraces everything, including the capacity for self-negation. Jung also argues that the limits of our language and our consciousness mean that we can speak only of a divine image that the human psyche can create, because we cannot conceive of the infinite God. To cope with the existence of this sublime force, we impose our own concepts on it.

Jung, like Kierkegaard, believes faith is "that twinkling of an eye in which the believer experiences the transcendental presence of God" (*Hebrew Encyclopaedia*, 1957, vol. 18, p. 691). Kierkegaard notes that when Abraham submits to the divine command "he achieves the leap to the transcendental cognition of God," whereas Jung defines this experience not as the inward essence of "the Knight of Faith" but as a numinous experience, tantamount to the experiencing of selfhood—recognition of the transcendent nature of the Self.

In conclusion, we offer a Jewish conception of the Binding, from Rabbi Abraham Isaac Kook's foreword to the prayerbook, *Olat Re'aya*:

The eternal wonder of the test of the Binding and its influence on the world generally originates in the full luminescence of life fulfilled at the occasion. The father is beset by none of the natural feelings of distraught and destroyed fatherly yearning; on the contrary, everything is alive and resplendent. [He acts] in the full knowledge that everything that lives, everything that rises up, everything, is meant to be obliterated, must be obliterated, and must be willing to forge the supreme attachment to the will and word of the supreme God, Creator of Heaven and Earth. . . . Although the virtue of compassion for the only son is so fine, ethical, and splendid, despite its compelling nature, such compassion must be denied in order to fulfill the word of the Lord and act wholeheartedly according to His will. Thus compassion itself achieves the highest dwelling-place, its place in the supreme reality of the will of the Omnipresent.

Everything visited upon that righteous man from the day he was born, and more generally everything visited upon the entire world, was in preparation for this terrible event, which provides a wonderful form for and sheds radiance upon the entire universe. (1968, p. 85)

At first view, Rabbi Kook's approach seems to be very close to Kierkegaard's. Closer scrutiny, however, reveals that it is based on a kabbalistic approach. Rabbi Kook construes Abraham's submission to the divine command as an elevation of the concept of human mercy (which should awaken in a father's heart as he views his bound son) to the ontological domain, and the kabbalistic symbol of Sefirah Tiferet, which is called compassion. The Binding brings about an emendation (Hebrew, *tikkun*) in the divinity itself. It is this that gives rise to the interaction between human being and divinity.

Thus, through his submission to the divine command, by means of his absolute faith, Abraham induces a change in a particular deficiency within God.

Bibliography

Barton, G. A. 1932. Circumcision [Semitic]. In J. Hastings, ed. *Encyclopedia of Religion and Ethics*. 2d ed. Edinburgh: T. and T. Clark.

Bialik, C. N. and Ravnitzki, J. C. 1951. "Ma'asei Avot" and other chapters. In *Sefer Ha'Aggada*. Tel Aviv: Dvir.

Bible: The Soncino Chumash. 1947. Hindhead, England: The Soncino Press.

Concise Oxford English Dictionary. 1942. London: Oxford University Press.

Dreifuss, G. 1965. A Psychological Study of Circumcision in Judaism. *Journal of Analytical Psychology* 10:1.

Even-Shoshan. 1969. *Hebrew Dictionary*. Jerusalem: Kirjat Sefer.

Finesinger, S. B. 1931–32. The Shofar. *Hebrew Union College Annual*, vols. 8–9. Cincinnati.

Gilboa, A. 1963. Yitshak [Isaac]. Tel Aviv: Ha'kibuts Ha'meuhad.

Ginzberg, L. 1954. *The Legends of the Jews*, vol. 2. Philadelphia: The Jewish Publication Society of America.

Gouri, H. 1966. Yerusha [Bequest]. In *Shoshanat Ruhot*. Tel Aviv: Ha'kibuts Ha'meuhad.

Hebrew Encyclopedia. 1957. Jerusalem, Tel Aviv: Ha'hevrah le Hotsa'at Entsyclopediot.

Hillel, A. 1973. Ein Ayil Tahtav [No Ram in His Stead]. In Ho'daya [Thanks]. Tel Aviv: Ha'kibuts Ha'meuhad.

Jung, C. G. 1973. *Memories, Dreams, Reflections*. Ed. A. Jaffe. New York: Pantheon Books.

———. 1971. *Psychological Types*. *CW* 6. Princeton, N.J.: Princeton University Press.

———. 1956. *Symbols of Transformation*. *CW* 5. Princeton, N.J.: Princeton University Press.

———. 1953. *Two Essays on Analytical Psychology*. *CW* 7. Princeton, N.J.: Princeton University Press.

Kierkegaard, S. 1909. *Fear and Trembling*. Tr. R. Payne. London: Oxford University Press.

Kook, A. I. 1968. Olat Re'aya [The Proof of the Burnt-Offering]. Jerusalem: Mosad Ha'rav Kook.

Meged, M. 1973. Ha'akedah [The Binding]. Published in a daily newspaper in Hebrew. Tr. H. Hofmann. Tel Aviv: Davar.

Midrash Genesis Rabbah. 1951. Ed. H. Freedman and M. Stein. London: The Soncino Press.

Neumann, E. 1969. *Depth Psychology and a New Ethics*. New York: Hodder and Stoughton.

———. 1963. Manheim, R., tr. *The Great Mother*. New York: Pantheon Books.

———. 1954. Hull, R. F. C., tr. *The Origins and History of Consciousness*. New York: Pantheon Books.

———. 1953. Der mystiche Mensch [Mystical Man]. In *Kultur-entwicklung und Religion*. Zurich: Rascher.

Otto, R. 1959. *The Idea of the Holy*. Tr. J. W. Harvey. New York: Penguin.

Rashi (Rabbi Shlomo Yitzhaqil of Troyes). *Pentateuch with Targum Onkelos, Haphtaroth and Rashi's Commentary*. Tr. and annotated by M. Rosenbaum and A. M. Silberman. New York: Hebrew Publishing Company.

Scheftelowitz, J. 1912. *Das Hoernermotiv in den Religionen*. Leipzig: Archiv fuer Religionswissenschaft.

Yizhar, S. 1967. Yimei Ziklag [The Days of Ziklag]. Excerpt. Tr. N. Greenwood. *Shdemot* 27. Tel Aviv.

Index